Ursuline Academy *to* Southwest School *of* Art & Craft
1851-2001

Maria Watson Pfeiffer

MAVERICK PUBLISHING COMPANY

MAVERICK PUBLISHING COMPANY

P.O. Box 6355, San Antonio, Texas 78209

Library of Congress Cataloging-in-Publication Data

Pfeiffer, Maria Watson, 1950-
School by the river : Ursuline Academy to Southwest School of
Art and Craft, 1851-2001 / Maria Watson Pfeiffer.
p. cm.
Includes bibliographical references and index.
ISBN 1-893271-19-6
1. Ursuline Academy (San Antonio, Tex.)‹History. 2. Southwest
Craft Center (San Antonio, Tex.)‹History. 3. Southwest School of
Art and Craft (San Antonio, Tex.)‹History. I. Title.
LD7251.S2972 P447 2001
373.764'351--dc21
2001004852

Design by Barbara Mathews Whitehead

Frontispiece: Ursuline Academy circa 1915
Ursuline Center Collection, Crystal City, Missouri

CONTENTS

Foreword / IX

CHAPTER ONE
The Ursulines: 1851-1951 / 1

CHAPTER TWO
Saving the Landmarks: 1952-1965 / 57

CHAPTER THREE
Inheritors of a Creative Legacy: 1965-1970 / 81

CHAPTER FOUR
The Art and Craft of Preservation: 1970-1975 / 113

CHAPTER FIVE
Beyond Beginnings: 1976-2001 / 141

The Founders / 181

The Southwest School of Art and Craft / 183

Bibliography / 189

Index / 191

DEDICATION

THOSE who visit the Southwest School of Art and Craft are invariably charmed and amazed by this peaceful oasis in the heart of San Antonio's bustling downtown. Indeed, a stroll through the tree-shaded grounds on the banks of the meandering San Antonio River transports the visitor back to an earlier time. The place is tranquil and, even on the hottest of Texas days, seems cooler than the surrounding city. The casual visitor can sense, though perhaps not know, that this place has survived through no accident. The school of creative excellence that today attracts students of all ages was envisioned by volunteers who worked tirelessly to make it a reality. In the process they became the stewards of this convent built by French missionaries in the middle nineteenth century, operated by the Ursuline sisters until 1965, and saved from certain destruction by those dedicated to the architectural and cultural heritage of their city.

Even in the early twenty-first century, newcomers to San Antonio may still be struck by the close interrelationships of people and institutions across the community. This is the legacy of a city that remained more like a small town well into its maturity. The story of the Ursuline Academy reflects the intricacies of San Antonio at its best—from the construction and operation of the school, to the survival of its buildings, to the founding and flourishing of the Southwest School of Art and Craft. It is a story with three themes—education, historic preservation, and love of artistic invention—that merged to produce and preserve this unique place. It is also the story of three groups of women who labored, each in their own time and way, to make this place what it is today.

It is to those women that this book is dedicated.

FOREWORD

THIS book, whose words flow through the pages like the river that binds us, is a story about ideas that became reality. It is a story about vision and courage, struggle and persistence, innovation and success. It is a story about permanence and change, power and influence, and about people in our own community who make a difference in our lives and who set standards that raise our city's consciousness. Not only does this book tell the story of the Ursuline Academy, but in its telling it also uncovers the story of a city and its people.

Those familiar limestone buildings on Augusta Street, with an old world air about them, are integral to San Antonio's fabric today. They began with an idea in the 1840s when Bishop John Marie Odin recognized that San Antonio did not have a school for the education of the town's young women. With that thought in mind, and with uncanny foresight he purchased a piece of property. Wisely, he then engaged the assistance of strong and determined women of the Order of Saint Ursula. Buildings began to rise on the banks of the San Antonio River, and this city was never the same again. Its skyline had a new jewel in its crown, and when the doors to those buildings opened for the first time in 1851, San Antonio's young women could then expect an education like never before.

Woven from exhaustive research, this is as much the story of the development of our city and the mettle of its people as it is about the ups and downs that time and fate dealt the Ursuline Academy. At its most vulnerable, when change and circumstances had driven the good sisters and their mission to the north of town, it looked like the Ursuline buildings would not end well. At one point even demolition was feared. That's when another set of strong and determined women stepped in, and the road to saving the old landmark began. It was a long and hard battle, but it was San Antonio's women of vision who pulled the Ursuline out of the danger facing it and transformed it into the vibrant and dynamic center for art and craft it is today. There is a different profile to the old Ursuline, but its raison d'etre forges on stronger than ever.

It couldn't have been otherwise. If there is anything that gives San Antonio its starch, it is its women, many of whom were educated by those same sisters. It is so gratifying that on this one hundred and fiftieth anniversary of the founding of the Ursuline Academy its legacy of education lives on as the Southwest School of Art and Craft.

Dora Elizondo Guerra

Head of Reference
Daughters of the
Republic of Texas Library
at The Alamo
June 25, 2001

The URSULINES

1851-1951

T HE night was magnificent, lighted by the stars and moon, but otherwise the beginning was inauspicious. A group of weary travelers—seven Ursuline nuns accompanied by Father Claude Marie Dubuis, pastor of the Alsatian community of Castroville—arrived in San Antonio late on the evening of September 14, 1851, to begin their work. They had braved a remote wilderness to fulfill the vision of Bishop John Marie Odin—the establishment of San Antonio's first Catholic school.

The sprawling state of Texas had been admitted to the Union only five years earlier, and its largest inland city was San Antonio, founded on the Spanish frontier in 1718. In the 40 years prior to the sisters' arrival, the city had survived battles between the Spanish and Mexican armies and the Mexican and Texan armies, Indian invasions, and cholera epidemics. A visitor to San Antonio in early 1846 described it as having a somewhat "foreign appearance, altogether dissimilar to any other Texas city . . . the entire place gave the impression of decay, and apparently at one time had seen better and more brilliant days."[1]

The parish church in this predominantly Catholic town was collapsing, and there were no organized schools, either religious or secular, to educate the children. Bishop Odin reasoned that a Catholic school would fill this void and expand the Church's influence on the frontier.

The Ursuline sisters' challenge was clear from the outset of their journey. Four sisters boarded a ship in New Orleans on September 7, 1851, for the three-day trip to Galveston, Texas. There they rested for a day at the state's first Ursuline convent, established in 1847. The group, joined by Father Dubuis and three of their Galveston sisters, boarded stagecoaches for the grueling trip across the Texas coastal plain. Soaked by torrential, late summer rains and jostled along muddy, rutted roads, the sisters arrived in San Antonio by moonlight to take up residence in a scorpion-infested structure with broken windows and no furniture. While Father Dubuis solicited mattresses and other supplies and the sisters cleaned the house, it must have occurred to them that this was not the end of a long journey, but only its beginning.

Catholic Missionaries on the Texas Frontier

In reality the journey had begun 11 years earlier while Texas was still a republic. In March 1837, one year after Texas won its independence from Mexico, Catholics led by John Joseph Linn of Victoria complained to Bishop Anthony Blanc of New Orleans that the Church in Texas had been neglected while under the jurisdiction of the Diocese of Monterrey, Mexico.[2] Few priests remained in the region following years of political unrest, war with Mexico, and economic turmoil, and Linn and his fellow petitioners asked Bishop Blanc to send missionaries to Texas.[3] Their concerns were advanced to Pope Gregory XVI, and the Vatican subsequently instructed Blanc to send a representative to Texas to study the situation. On March 30, 1838, Father John Timon, a member of the Vincentian missionary order, was assigned to ascertain "the present state of things and the future prospects of religion" in Texas.[4]

John Timon left the Vincentian St. Mary's of the Barrens Seminary in Missouri and arrived in Galveston on December 27, 1839. He met in Houston with officers of the Republic of Texas, including Sam Houston, Mirabeau Lamar, and David Burnet.[5] Timon was also briefed by Senator Juan N. Seguin and Representative José Antonio Navarro, both of San Antonio, who cautioned him that a trip to their town was ill advised because of the presence of Indians and Mexican guerrillas along the route. Their account of conditions at San Antonio's San Fernando Church convinced Timon that it was administered two immoral priests, one described "as scandalous and concubinous," and he recommended that Texas Catholics be removed from the jurisdiction of Monterrey.[6] Bishop Blanc agreed, and on April 12, 1840, he appointed John Timon the prefect apostolic of Texas. Timon, in turn, nominated his friend and colleague, John Marie Odin, as his vice prefect.[7]

John Timon had met the French-born priest John Marie Odin 15 years earlier in 1825 when they traveled 1,200 miles together through Missouri and central Arkansas conducting a survey of Catholicism. At the time of his appointment as prefect apostolic, Timon was rector of the Vicentian's Missouri seminary and was therefore unable to perform extended missionary work. He knew and respected Odin, however, and immediately sent him to Texas.

The Ruins of War

San Antonio was still in ruins from the battles of the Texas Revolution when John Marie Odin arrived there on July 30, 1840.[8] Only four months earlier Texas troops had killed over 30 Comanches in the Council House Fight across the plaza from San Fernando Church.[9] Writing to his superiors, Odin estimated that there were about 1800 residents in San Antonio, all but 100 to 150 of whom were Mexicans. He decried the condition of the church building that had burned in 1828 and had been ruined further by the war of 1836, describing it as a decrepit ruin infested by swallows and bats and having "such a foul odor that it is impossible to enter in the morning without feeling like vomiting."[10] Seeking to restore credibility among the town's disaffected Catholics, Odin first dispatched the derelict priests and then began to repair San Fernando. On December 5, 1841, people flocked in from towns and ranches up to 30 miles away to celebrate the completion of the work with a Mass and bonfires in the town's two plazas.[11]

San Antonio's four outlying Spanish missions were similarly decayed.[12] Odin described Missions Espada and San Juan as "not very remarkable and almost entirely destroyed." He was, however, intrigued by Mission San José that he thought to be "especially beautiful" and Mission Concepción, whose site on the river he found "charming."

Father John Marie Odin visited San Antonio as a missionary in 1840 and purchased a 12-acre site on the San Antonio River for a Catholic school. Though he became the first bishop of Galveston, Odin remained committed to the education of San Antonio's children, and through his efforts the Ursuline convent opened in 1851. *Courtesy of the Catholic Archives of San Antonio.*

San Fernando Church was in ruins when Father John Marie Odin arrived in San Antonio in 1840. His restoration of the neglected building helped revive Catholicism and lay the foundation for the church's growth in the community. *Courtesy of the Witte Museum, San Antonio, Texas.*

Apparently already envisioning a Catholic school on the frontier, Odin wrote to his bishop about Concepción, "what a delightful place for a boarding school for young girls!" [13]

While he lamented the condition of the Church's property, Odin purchased additional land in San Antonio. Only seven weeks after arriving, he wrote in his journal that he had given a note to Ludovic Colquhoun for a 12-acre lot.[14] Like Mission Concepción that Odin so admired, the newly acquired property was on the meandering San Antonio River. Though Odin did not record his rationale for purchasing the land, he did indeed have a plan.

Father Odin wrote often and eloquently to his colleagues about the spiritual and physical condition of the Church in San Antonio, most of all lamenting the lack of religious teaching. After a year in Texas he wrote to Father Timon, "the more I consider the needs of San Antonio, the more I

remain convinced that the interests of religion call for the establishment of a convent here."[15] Protestants were already sending their children to Odin's catechism classes, and he speculated that they would also send them to a convent school to be raised in the Catholic faith. Though Odin never wavered from this vision, it would be ten years before it was realized.

Father John Marie Odin found Mission Concepción, one of San Antonio's four outlying Spanish missions, to be "charming" and believed that it would make an excellent site for a boarding school for girls. *Courtesy of the Witte Museum.*

The First Bishop in Texas

John Odin's first years in the Republic of Texas were filled with challenges and his determination to succeed did not go unnoticed. Within two years of Odin's arrival, the Republic of Texas was elevated from a mission to a vicariate-apostolic, and Father Odin was given the authority of a bishop and consecrated on March 6, 1842.[16]

The region was suffering a terrible drought, and Indian raids, inva-

sions from Mexico, and disease were ongoing problems. To overcome these adversities Odin constantly sought financial assistance from the Leopoldine Society and the Society for the Propagation of the Faith in Lyon, France.[17] He attempted to convey the magnitude of his charge by describing Texas as larger than France with a "sparse and poor population dispersed through this vast area."[18]

Funds and facilities were already inadequate when American and European immigrants began to arrive in the Republic of Texas in the mid-1840s, enticed by promises of free land and a new life. Though the new arrivals brought vitality and diversity to the region, they often settled on land provided by colonization companies far from established towns. Many of these immigrants were Catholic and non-English speaking, including the Alsatian families brought by Henri Castro to a new colony on the Medina River 25 miles west of San Antonio.[19]

Bishop Odin could not serve his growing flock with a meager budget and few priests, and he left for an extended trip to Europe in 1845 to recruit missionaries and raise money to support his work. Knowing that Henri Castro planned to bring another 600 families to Texas to join the 60 who had come in 1844, Odin requested 22 priests and 10 nuns, living expenses, and the assurance of funds to construct an Ursuline convent, church, hospital, and orphans home in Galveston.[20] In Lyon Odin's appeal was heard by Claude Marie Dubuis, a recently ordained

The Alsatian community of Castroville, 25 miles west of San Antonio was settled in 1844, and Bishop John Marie Odin recruited missionaries to serve the largely Catholic colony. *The Institute of Texan Cultures, courtesy of the Landmark Inn.*

priest, who volunteered to do missionary work in Texas. Odin overcame the objections of Dubuis' parents, and the young recruit began his journey to Texas on February 19, 1846, the day Texas joined the United States.

Opposite: Father Claude Marie Dubuis arrived in Texas as a missionary in 1847 and, four years later, accompanied the Ursuline sisters on their journey from Galveston to San Antonio. Dubuis worked tirelessly to assist the order and remained devoted to its work even after succeeding John Marie Odin as bishop of Galveston in 1862. *Courtesy of the Catholic Archives of San Antonio.*

In the Cause of Catholic Education: The Ursuline Order in Texas

Bishop Odin, Father Dubuis, eight other clerics, and three Ursuline sisters arrived in New Orleans on May 25, 1846. The Ursulines remained at their New Orleans convent, while Odin returned to Galveston and Dubuis traveled to St. Mary's of the Barrens Seminary in Missouri to learn English.[23] The bishop had been away from Galveston for almost a year, and was encouraged by the number of new colonists who had settled there during his absence. He soon made another trip to New Orleans and, in January 1847, returned with eight Ursuline nuns to open the first Catholic school in Texas. He wrote, "The establishment, I hope, will contribute much to the glory of God and salvation of souls in the apostolic vicarage of Texas."[21]

While in Europe in 1845, Bishop Odin had continued to promote his vision of a Catholic school in San Antonio. He described the town to his benefactors as "a land so beautiful and so healthful and where there would be such a great abundance of young people not only from

Bishop John Marie Odin leased the Alamo to the United States Army during the United States-Mexican War for use as a quartermaster depot. *Courtesy of the Witte Museum, San Antonio, Texas*

Texas but also from the whole western part of Mexico." [22] Writing to his friend and mentor, John Timon, Odin proposed restoring the church at the Alamo and building a school adjacent to the old mission. He estimated that the remaining ruins contained "more stones than necessary to construct a huge school." [23] These plans were put aside temporarily when Odin leased the Alamo to the United States Army to use as a supply depot for the duration of the United States-Mexican War. [24]

When Father Claude Marie Dubuis returned to Galveston from Missouri in January 1847, Bishop Odin assigned him to Henri Castro's growing colony near San Antonio. [25] Odin wrote to both Bishop Blanc in New Orleans and the Society for the Propagation of the Faith in France in April 1847 that Dubuis was doing well and that "our small community of Ursulines is enjoying excellent health." [26] Though Odin, in his letters, continued to envision the Alamo as "an excellent locale for a school large enough for all the children of San Antonio," he had, in reality, already begun constructing the buildings that would become San Antonio's Ursuline convent. [27]

Hesitating No Longer

Bishop Odin had become increasingly concerned that Protestants were undermining the Catholic Church in San Antonio by establishing their own schools. Just as Odin had been sent to Texas in 1840 by the Catholic Church, Reverend John McCullough had been assigned by the Presbyterian Church that same year as the first moderator of the Texas Presbytery.[28] McCullough was also a committed missionary and teacher, and he opened a day school that by 1848 had 50 students. He wrote, "If I were to commence a free school, I could have at least 500 Mexican children in daily attendance."[29]

McCullough's work in San Antonio was augmented by the Bible Society of New York that sent Reverend Ramon Montsalvage, a former Spanish monk, to open a school for poor Mexican children. The *Presbyterian Herald* in May 1849 reported, "the Catholic bishop has recently been here, devising a means to prevent his [Montsalvage's] influence. The priests are afraid to manifest the Catholic spirit towards

Artist William G.M. Samuel painted the west side of San Antonio's Main Plaza in 1849, two years before the Ursuline sisters arrived to open their school. *Courtesy of the Witte Museum, San Antonio, Texas.*

[9]

Reverend John McCullough conducted missionary work in San Antonio for the Presbyterian Church during the 1840s, while Bishop John Marie Odin was constructing churches and schools for the Catholic Church. *Courtesy of the San Antonio Public Library.*

American Protestants, but have not failed to show the spirit of papacy towards the Spaniard, by warning the Mexicans against him publicly and in private. They have become alarmed for the safety of Catholicism here, and have contracted for the building of a large nunnery and school."[30]

Indeed, when Bishop Odin visited San Antonio in September 1848, he found several schools operated by the Bible Society. When he warned parents of this threat to Catholicism, they, in turn, told him that he needed to provide alternative schools. Odin wrote with alarm to his supporters, "The Bible Society of New York is going to great lengths to poison the minds of the poor Mexicans still living in Texas."

Though he lacked funds Odin was determined to build his long-awaited convent. He had purchased the site on the San Antonio River in 1840, but "war and my poverty had prevented me from building on it the convent for which it was intended. At the sight of the danger threatening the children . . . I felt I could no longer hesitate."[31] Odin plunged himself further into debt, borrowing 20,000 francs to build two Catholic schools—one for girls and one for boys. After almost ten years, his dream would finally become a reality.

Convent on the River

Bishop Odin selected François Giraud, a French surveyor and architect, to construct his school for girls. Born in Charleston, South Carolina, to French immigrant parents, Giraud studied in France and came to Texas in 1847 when his father was appointed French consul.[32] Giraud and his younger brother Theodore, an architect, were soon working regularly for the French-dominated Catholic Church in Louisiana and Texas.[33]

F. Giraud, as he was called, received directions to proceed with the San Antonio convent in late 1848, and by January 1849 the foundation was under construction. Giraud wrote to Odin in Galveston that "the stone foundations are moving forward and are favorably done with good materials."[34] Building supplies were ordered, but they arrived slowly. The limestone was quarried locally and the wood was shipped from Bastrop, a town northeast of San Antonio. Giraud constantly worried to Odin that funds were inadequate to complete the masonry work that was

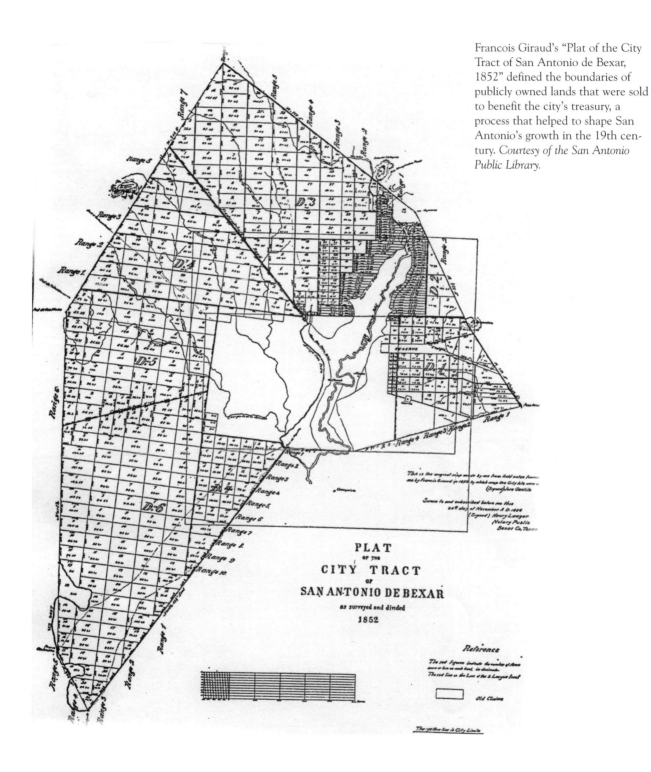

Francois Giraud's "Plat of the City Tract of San Antonio de Bexar, 1852" defined the boundaries of publicly owned lands that were sold to benefit the city's treasury, a process that helped to shape San Antonio's growth in the 19th century. *Courtesy of the San Antonio Public Library.*

François Giraud, trained in France as an engineer, designed and built many structures for the Catholic Church in Texas, including the earliest building at San Antonio's Ursuline convent. *The Institute of Texan Cultures, courtesy of the San Antonio Conservation Society.*

François Pierre Giraud, more often called Francis or simply F. Giraud, was born in Charleston, South Carolina, on June 1, 1818, to French immigrant parents. He received his degree in engineering from the Ecole Centrale des Arts et Manufactureres in Paris in 1841 and returned to teach at Mount St. Mary's College in Maryland. Giraud left with his family in 1845 for Texas where his father, also named François, had been appointed French consul. In Texas F. Giraud did not lack for jobs, and both he and his younger brother Theodore, an architect, often worked for the Catholic Church. As early as March 1848, Theodore was designing buildings and furnishings for Bishop Odin in Galveston and for Bishop Blanc in New Orleans. F. Giraud served as San Antonio city engineer from 1849 until 1853 and as mayor from 1872 to 1877. As city engineer Giraud completed a survey that delineated the boundaries of the city's eighteenth century town tract. That survey was used to identify city-owned lands that were either reserved for public use or available for sale to generate funds for the city treasury. Among the reserves designated by Giraud was the area surrounding San Pedro Springs, today known as San Pedro Springs Park. For the Catholic Church Giraud surveyed the Spanish missions and completed plans for St. Mary's Church in 1855 and the renovation of San Fernando Church in 1868. François Giraud died in 1877 at the age of 59, and his funeral Mass was celebrated at San Fernando Cathedral. Giraud was eulogized as "a gentleman always; a Christian in the fullest . . . A grand old man, by his many virtues commanding respect and admiration of all." But above all François Giraud was the person who had defined the public face of the Catholic Church in San Antonio.

JULES POINSARD. BUILDER BY CONTRACT. FLORES Street, opposite A. Martinez. Has the honor of informing the public, that he is prepared to undertake, at moderate rates, such buildings as may be entrusted to him, and also interior and exterior decoration. Masonry, Carpenter's and Cabinet work. Printing, Sculpture and papering. Drafting, Architecture, and laying off of gardens attended to. Pise work at $1.75 per perch; and also a lot of parlour statues for sale.   8·3m

Jules Poinsard advertised his services, including *pise*, or rammed earth construction, the technique that he used to construct the first building at the Ursuline convent. *San Antonio* Texan.

scheduled to begin about the third week in February.[35] To cover his expenses Giraud borrowed money from local Catholics, including François Guilbeau, José Cassiano, Bryan Callaghan, and Edward Dwyer.[36]

Perhaps it was Giraud's concern for cost that led him to construct the building's walls of local clay, using a method called rammed earth or *pisé de terre*.[37] His choice of material might also have resulted from ongoing anti-Catholic prejudice. Writing in 1852 about the building's construction, Sister Augustine Joseph stated that the Catholic Church "was refused permission to draw stones from the Government quarry, it is said, thro' prejudiced motives."[38] Clay used in *pisé de terre* construction was readily available from the creek and river bottoms in and around the city and, though less durable, was much cheaper than quarried stone. There was also a skilled practitioner of the *pisé* technique in San Antonio, another Frenchman, Jules Poinsard.

Jules Poinsard was born in 1814 in Paris, graduated with honors from the Ecole des Arts et Métiers in Chalon, and came to Texas in 1846.[39] He was apparently already a trained builder when he arrived in San Antonio and has been credited with constructing some of the town's most prominent buildings, including the imposing 1847 home of French merchant François Guilbeau, one of the convent's financiers.[40] Poinsard was listed on the 1850 Texas census as an architect and, in 1855, advertised as a "builder by contract" who did masonry, carpentry, cabinetry, and "*pisé* work for $1.75 per perch."[41] As a Frenchman and a skilled builder, Jules Poinsard was a logical choice to assist in building the convent for F. Giraud.

Giraud was apparently pleased with Poinsard's work and, in early

The first academy building, designed by François Giraud and constructed of *pise de terre* by Jules Poinsard, was completed in 1851 and enlarged in 1854. *Southwest School of Art and Craft.*

March 1849, reported to Bishop Odin that "the masonry is already coming along and is of a superior quality; the clay could not be better."[42] The project proceeded quickly, and by mid-March the walls and roof were erected and door and window frames were installed.[43] Still, a good deal remained to be done, including construction of a staircase, completion of the fireplaces, and the installation and painting of doors, windows, and flooring. Of greater importance the clay building required plastering to protect it from periodic rains, and the site needed to be fenced to keep out intruders and ranging livestock. Progress was slow, and it was not until February 23, 1851, that Giraud was able to report that the convent was nearing completion. "There only remains the finishing of the fence on the north side to complete the cloister wall."[44]

Impatiently Awaited

Bishop Odin was a master of inspiration and persuasion. In 1847 he had successfully convinced the Ursuline Order to purchase land on

Poinsard's Folly

The correspondence between François Giraud and Bishop Odin disputes the long-told story of Poinsard's Folly. This legend maintained that Poinsard emigrated from France to Texas, leaving behind his reluctant lover, and in Texas built an impressive house to entice her to join him, only to be disappointed. The building, known both as the Ursuline First Academy and Poinsard's Folly, was indeed constructed to satisfy a dream, but it was that of Odin's long-envisioned girl's school, not Poinsard's unrequited love. Giraud's letters do, however, shed some light on the Poinsard's romantic tale. Giraud advised Bishop Odin in March 1850 that he had sent $40 to Poinsard's "lady" in France. Perhaps Poinsard's earnings allowed the woman to join him in San Antonio. Whatever the case, the 1850 United States census of Texas recorded Jules Poinsard and Hannah Poinsard, both age 32 and born in France, living together in San Antonio. It is only an assumption that Hannah Poinsard was in fact Jules Poinsard's "lady." What is known is that Jules Poinsard never owned the Ursuline property and that he only served as a subcontractor to François Giraud in the building of the first convent building. Poinsard enjoyed a successful career and traveled throughout Texas constructing pisé buildings for the United States Army. He became eccentric in his later years, but when he died on August 5, 1885, in Santa Rosa Infirmary without survivors, the newspaper noted that his funeral was attended by the town's "most prominent French citizens."

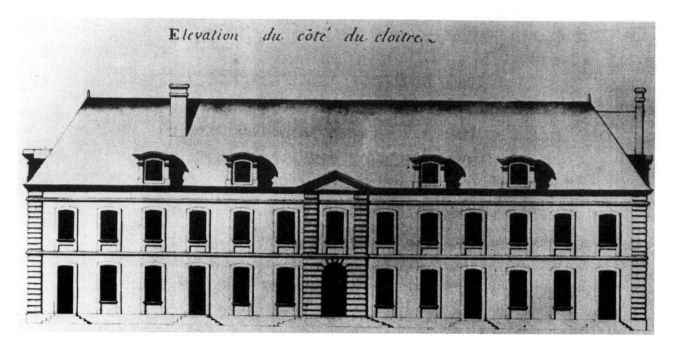

Elevation du côté du cloitre.

The first convent constructed by the Ursuline Order in New Orleans in 1745 was replaced in 1752 by this structure that still stands. The building's design is reminiscent of the dormitory at the Ursuline's San Antonio convent. *Samuel Wilson Jr. Collection, courtesy of Koch and Wilson Architects.*

Galveston Island. There the sisters established the first Catholic school in Texas under the most adverse circumstances, but after only four years the school was flourishing. Now, with his San Antonio convent nearing completion, Odin again recruited the Ursuline sisters.

F. Giraud, writing to Odin of the building's completion in February 1851, indicated that the sisters' arrival was "impatiently awaited" and pressed Odin to send them soon.[45] San Antonio had only one priest, who was already struggling to meet parishioners' needs, and without more help he would be unable to minister to the new school. Odin's negotiations with the Ursuline Order were tedious and protracted, and he had not received an answer from the New Orleans convent before embarking on an extended trip to Europe to secure more missionaries and funding. Proud of his accomplishments to date but frustrated with the sisters' lack of response, he turned to Archbishop Anthony Blanc in New Orleans for assistance. "By dint of sacrifices I have finally succeeded in having a convent built in San Antonio." He implored Blanc to intercede on his behalf with the Ursulines. "I hope, Monseigneur, that you will have the kindness to confirm their departure and to encourage them in such a meritorious work. It is distressing to see how many poor children are lost in San Antonio for lack of a good school."[46]

The coat of arms for the Order of St. Ursula carries the motto Soli Deo Gloria, "only to the Glory of God." *Ursusline Provincialate, Crystal City Missouri.*

The Ursuline Order

The Ursuline Order was founded in Italy in 1535 by St. Angela Merici, the daughter of an Italian farmer. Angela had lost her parents and sister by the time she was a teenager and joined the Third Order of St. Francis. As a young woman she had a vision of the heavens opening, revealing processions of angels and young girls, singing and playing musical instruments. Recognizing her sister in the dream, Angela took this vision as her inspiration to open a school to instruct young girls in the Catholic religion. She believed that educated and religious women were a strong social force and organized the Company of St. Ursula, a group of 12 women named for St. Ursula, a fourth-century martyr and patroness of education. St. Angela's teaching abilities were officially recognized in 1612 by Pope Paul V, and the group was designated the Order of St. Ursula, a cloistered order that performed apostolic work through the education of young women. St. Angela instructed that "If with change of times and circumstances, it becomes necessary to make fresh rules or to alter anything, then do it with prudence, after taking good advice." This good counsel carried the sisters from Italy to France, throughout Europe, England, Ireland, and by 1639 to Quebec, Canada. Eighty-six years later, in 1727, the sisters arrived in New Orleans as the first community of women religious in Louisiana. When Bishop Odin accompanied the first Ursuline sisters to Galveston in 1847, the order had been working in North America for over 200 years.

The Ursuline sisters announced the opening of their new school in a bilingual advertisement published in the San Antonio *Ledger*.

Bishop Odin left the country not knowing when the Ursulines would arrive in San Antonio. He was in Europe when Archbishop Blanc confirmed on August 26, 1851, that Mother Superior St. Marie Trouard (Constance Trouard), her mother assistant and abbot, Sister St. Antoine (Sarah Monaghan), and lay sisters Sister St. Isidore (Rosalie Entienne) and Sister St. Alexis (Lise Portier) would leave New Orleans for San Antonio.[47] Less than two weeks later the sisters were on a ship bound for their new life in Texas. They arrived in Galveston where they were joined by Father Dubuis and Sisters Angela, St. Marie, and Xavier and then departed for San Antonio. Three weeks after the trip began, the sisters caught their first glimpse of San Antonio.

A year after the sisters' arrival, their story was recounted by Sister Mary Patrick Joseph, an Irish Ursuline who arrived at the convent in July 1852. "On the eve of the Exaltation of the holy Cross, 1851, the Sisters arrived at San Antonio about ten o'clock on Saturday night. They drove to the Convent & when they alighted, they were obliged to walk thro' grass a foot & a half high, which trimmed & filled the pathway to the house. Arrived at the hall-door & that by moonlight, they saw the hall filled with mortar, rubbish, window blinds, sashes, etc. They stumbled over these & ascended the staircase & entered the room now occupied as a Dormitory & found there was absolutely nothing . . . They could see the starry heavens thro' the apertures in the roof, & the room was without windows"[48]

The sisters were greeted with interest and curiosity. Townspeople provided food and furnishings, and young boys climbed trees to peer through the undraped windows. The convent was barely habitable and the sisters reported that "the honest architect boasts of having extracted two or three thousands piasters more than he should have got from Monsignor."[49] Father Dubuis, who had constructed his own church in Castroville, worked with an Irish carpenter, Ned Walshe, to complete the job apparently left unfinished by François Giraud and Jules Poinsard.[50] They installed doors and windows and, with a $500 donation from the Ursuline sisters in New Orleans, built a gallery on the convent's north side.[51] Walshe remarked about his work at the San Antonio convent, "God brought me here to remedy this botched carpentry."[52] Of Father Dubuis the sisters wrote, "Often when he returned from the Missions, harassed with fatigue, hunger, and thirst, he would immediately take his trowel which he held with one hand while with the other he ate corn pancakes that our Sister St. Alexis had cooked."[53] Dubuis was described as "everything to this Institute since its establishment—he is carpenter, painter, mason, etc. and then so zealous for the instruction of the dear children."[54]

Undaunted by their adversities and with Dubuis' assistance, the sisters miraculously convened the first classes ever held by a Catholic religious order in San Antonio on November 3, 1851, only six weeks after arriving in the city. "Early in the morning the parents began to arrive with their children—Americans, French, Germans, Mexicans, etc." As there was only one bridge across the San Antonio River at that time, they had traveled a circuitous route to the school along Main Street (today's Commerce) to Acequia Street (today's Main Avenue) and to the convent's west doorway. There, they entered through the high stone wall to begin their new life. On that first day, Sister St. Marie, the mother superior, received payment from the new students "and between the melange of languages and names, she thought she would lose her intellect." [55] The girls were put into classes according to language and ability, and the Ursuline sisters began to teach on the site where they would remain for the next 114 years.

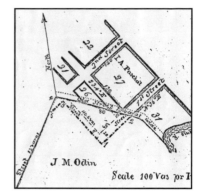

Bishop John Marie Odin sold one and a quarter acres of the Ursuline convent site in 1851 to developers I.A. Paschal and Nat Lewis for their subdivision named Upper San Antonio. *Bexar County Deed Records.*

Effecting Immense Good

Bishop Odin had left for Europe in 1851 confident that San Antonio's Ursuline convent would open and be successful. His assessment was correct, and upon returning to Texas in 1852 he was able to report that the convents in both San Antonio and Galveston were flourishing and inspiring confidence in parents.[56] While in Europe Odin had recruited additional sisters for his mission. In July 1852 Sisters Mary Patrick Joseph and Mary Augustine Joseph arrived in San Antonio from the Ursuline convent in Waterford, Ireland, to join their French sisters. They settled into their new home that they described as "small but very well arranged" and immersed themselves in learning Spanish, one of four languages used at the school together with French, German, and English.[57] They were taught by a local girl named Rudecinda de la Garza, a descendant of Spanish Canary Islanders who settled in San Antonio in 1731. As an accomplished linguist who was

LETTER

From our dear Sisters Missioners
San Antonio-Feast of St. Martha-July 29th 1852

✝
J.M.J.

My beloved Mother

We have, thank God arrived safely at
our destination, after a very tiresome journey, of which
dear Sister M. Patrick has given the details. Our new
home is far more comfortable than we expected; & as
you may suppose, we met a warm welcome from our
dear Revd. Mother, & from all here.

Above: Sisters Mary Patrick Joseph and Mary Augustine Joseph wrote to their mother convent in Waterford, Ireland, about their arrival in San Antonio in July 1852. *Courtesy of the Daughters of the Republic of Texas Library.*

Opposite: St. Mary's School for boys, designed by François Giraud, opened in August 1852 on the banks of the San Antonio River just a short distance south of the Ursuline convent. *Courtesy of the Witte Museum, San Antonio, Texas.*

fluent in both Spanish and French, she taught the sisters and also translated for them. The convent had been open only four years when Rudecinda de la Garza joined the Ursuline Order and became Sister Mary Magdalen on September 13, 1855. Fourteen years later the sisters' Spanish teacher would become their mother superior.

Kate Campbell Merritt Clarkson recalled entering the Ursuline in 1851 when she was eight years old. "We thought it was a beautiful place for it had big pecan trees on the river instead of a fence. On the north side there was a field where all sorts of garden produce were (sic) raised, then there was a garden and an orchard and flowers everywhere." She remembered learning "old fashioned things" like reading, spelling, writing, and arithmetic, as well as needlepoint, penmanship, art and etiquette.[58] The first students at the convent school were arranged in three sections, and in addition to the courses remembered by Kate Clarkson, they were taught exposition, geography, English grammar and parsing, astronomy, and history. Spanish-speaking students also learned Spanish grammar and English.[59] The sisters were soon turning away students for lack of room, and, fearing additional debt, Bishop Odin was reluctant to expand the convent. Sister Mary Patrick Joseph wrote to the Waterford convent, "You must pray San Antonio [St. Anthony] to send means to enlarge the house & then please God, we shall have full schools."[60]

In August 1852 Odin wrote another of his frequent letters soliciting funds from the Society for the Propagation of the Faith. He reported, "The Ursuline sisters established here since last October have already affected immense good among the little girls who have attended their school."[61] As in the past Odin painted a dire picture of education in San Antonio. He estimated that only 200 of San Antonio's 7,000 Catholics were able to read and write and that additional funds from Europe were needed to strengthen his mission and win more converts. Odin's letter of August 25, 1852, preceded the opening of his school for boys by only five days. St. Mary's School, operated by the Brothers of Mary, was only a short distance south of the Ursuline convent on the San Antonio River. Odin described it as a "bulwark against the efforts of Protestantism" and complained mightily that free schools paid for by the municipal treasury had forced both the brothers and sisters to admit more free students than they could afford.[62]

Newspaper publisher James Pearson Newcomb espoused the anti-Catholic, Know-Nothing cause and used his publication as a forum to denounce the Ursuline convent and advance the cause of public education. *Alamo Star.*

> ☞ The public schools will be re-opened on Monday, Sept. 4th, on the east side of the river near the new bridge. All four schools will be together in the same building, but in different rooms.

An Admirably Conducted School

The Ursuline Academy had 80 students and had been operating only 17 months when Father Dubuis toured a reporter for the San Antonio *Ledger* through the school. The reporter was impressed. "We must confess that we were surprised to find so large and so admirably conducted a school in our midst . . . to our own citizens we usually say there can no longer be any excuse for sending your daughters from home for an education; and to those abroad, desiring to avail themselves of the advantages of a good English and Classical School, we can say that we know no better institution than that of the Ursulines in this city." He described the school buildings as "large and airy and beautifully located on the banks of the San Antonio River."[63]

Father Dubuis was buoyed by the school's success and wrote to Bishop Odin in June 1853 that he was "without the least anxiety for the nuns." A generous donation had allowed Dubuis to pay the convent's debts and to buy provisions for six months.[64] He retained his optimism in spite of anti-Catholic sentiments that were still prevalent in the community. The Ursuline convent, lauded by the local press in 1853, became the subject of public criticism when James Pearson Newcomb began to publish the *Alamo Star* in March 1854.[65] Newcomb espoused the anti-Catholic Know-Nothing cause and used his platform to rail against the convent in October 1854. His paper gave extensive coverage to public education, reporting in 1855 that at least 100 children attended public schools.[66]

San Antonians were apparently undeterred by Newcomb's negative rhetoric and continued to send their girls to be educated by the sisters.

In October 1854 Odin reported that the school had 20 boarding students and nearly 100 day students and that there was no place to house more children.[67] Father Dubuis was confident enough to hire builder Francis C. Schmitt to construct a new stone building in 1854, and this addition to the academy's first building provided the sisters with a small chapel, kitchen, and more classroom and dormitory space.[68]

Texas troops gathered on Main Plaza for the surrender of the United States forces at the outset of the Civil War. *Courtesy of the Daughters of the Republic of Texas Library.*

The Consequences of War

The beginning of the Civil War in Texas was marked by the surrender of Major General David E. Twiggs, commander of United States troops in Texas, to representatives of the state on San Antonio's Main

Plaza on February 16, 1861. Though fighting did not take place in San Antonio, a blockade of the Gulf coast hampered trade and strained the state's economy. While some residents left to fight for the Confederacy, others fled to Union states, Europe, or Mexico to conduct their business, or to avoid conscription.

Shortly before the outbreak of war, Archbishop Anthony Blanc died, and five days after the war began, on April 19, 1861, Bishop Odin was appointed his successor. Odin and Father Dubuis were traveling together in France during October of the following year when they received word of Dubuis' appointment as the second Bishop of Galveston. After being consecrated by Odin at a service held in Lyon, the new bishop returned to Texas.

Though Claude Marie Dubuis had been elevated to Bishop of Galveston, San Antonio's Ursuline convent always held a special place for him. He had nurtured the sisters' endeavors since their arrival in September 1851, and during the Civil War he bestowed a great blessing on the convent by sending Father Etienne Buffard to serve as its chaplain. Much like Dubuis in his early career, Buffard labored tirelessly to improve the convent buildings. He remained there for 32 years and, when he died in 1896, was buried beneath the floor of the chapel that he helped to build.[69]

The Ursuline sisters relied on old friendships to sustain their school throughout the Civil War. Though Sister St. Marie wrote to Archbishop Odin in May 1864 that "all the rich families have gone to Mexico," the convent nonetheless had 172 children and the number was increasing daily.[70] From the outset the school had attracted students from Mexico, and these close relationships served the sisters well during the war. The convent's total assets of $14,000 were reportedly sent to Governor Madero in Saltillo, Mexico, who used the funds to purchase goods for the sisters and students. When the Ursuline convent in Galveston was damaged by shelling and converted to a hospital for the duration of the war, the San Antonio convent provided a stable environment for students and a quiet haven for those who fled hostilities on the coast. [71]

At the end of the Civil War in 1865, Governor Madero reportedly returned the balance of the sisters' funds with a $200 donation to assist the school. Sister St. Marie wrote on August 19, 1865, to Odin that "their school lacked for nothing during the war." She mused about the

uncertainties of Reconstruction and the effects of emancipation but looked to the future. The sisters, she stated, "were going to build a place for themselves and give up what they used before to the children."[72] Soon, ground was broken for a new chapel and dormitory building.

The Rapid March of Improvement

San Antonio prospered in the post-war period. Father Buffard reported to Archbishop Odin in early 1866 that new stores were continually being built in San Antonio and that there were over 600 retail establishments at the time. Just as the commercial interests of the city prospered, so did the educational efforts of the Ursulines. The school had 60 boarders and 160 day students, and now the sisters turned their attention to the necessity of expansion.[73]

Building materials were scarce and expensive in San Antonio after the Civil War. Nonetheless, Bishop Dubuis reported to Archbishop Odin in November 1865 that construction would begin on a new dormitory. After 14 years the sisters and children would have separate quarters.[74] Supervision of the dormitory project fell to Father Buffard who proved to be a resourceful, though occasionally frustrated, overseer. He ordered hard-to-come-by supplies for builder Francis Schmitt

The Ursuline convent dormitory, built by contractor Francis Schmitt in 1866 following the Civil War, was topped with a three-sided clock tower facing south, east, and west. Theories regarding the missing north face range from the scarcity of development to the sister's reluctance to give the time of day to the Yankees, recalling the recent hostilities between north and south. *Courtesy of the Daughters of the Republic of Texas Library.*

and proudly reported that he had acquired wood from Florida "at a bargain." Buffard also predicted that the project would cause him to "lose what little priestliness" he had.

Bishop Dubuis reported after visiting San Antonio in late 1865 that "the walls of the big building for the Ursulines were seven feet high," and by early 1866 the first arch of the east corridor was under construction. When Dubuis left for France in mid-1866, he deposited $4,000 with Archbishop Odin to assure completion of the building, and the dormitory's cornerstone was laid and blessed on September 14, 1866.[75]

Within days of the cornerstone ceremony, San Antonio experienced a terrible outbreak of cholera, and on October 11 the San Antonio *Daily Herald* reported that the disease had claimed one of the dormitory's construction workers. "The inmates of the establishment, sixty in number, have hitherto had perfect immunity from disease, and there is reason to hope that the precautions taken to secure a continuance will be sufficient."[76] The convent, however, was not immune. Writing in his memoirs Dr. Ferdinand Peter Herff recounted how his grandfather Dr. Ferdinand Herff ministered to the Ursuline sisters during this time. He remembered sadly that the epidemic eventually claimed 14 sisters who were buried in the small cemetery, located east of the convent.[77]

Construction in San Antonio continued in spite of this turmoil, and

A new chapel attributed to François Giraud was completed in 1868, and for the first time, townspeople could worship at the Ursuline convent. *Courtesy of the Daughters of the Republic of Texas Library.*

when the *Daily Herald* reported the City's annual accomplishments at the end of 1866 the writer was gratified to note three new buildings for educational purposes. In addition to St. Mary's Hall (the new Episcopal female school), the German English School had expanded, and "a very large addition to the Convent Building" had been completed.[78] To provide better access to the convent, a new footbridge was built over the San Antonio River in October 1866.[79]

Attention then turned to erecting a new chapel to replace the small worship space that had been used by the sisters since 1853. The cornerstone was laid on January 20, 1867, and in April 1868 the *Daily Herald* described the "magnificent" building to be nearly complete.[80] For the first time the public could attend Mass at the convent.[81] Visitors entered and worshipped on the west side of the chapel, while the cloistered sisters sat shielded from view on the north side. They were called to Mass by a French-made clock that chimed the hour from high atop the new dormitory. The timepiece was declared a great convenience for the upper portion of the city, though no note was taken of its missing north face. It has long been speculated that sparse development north of the convent did not justify the expense of a fourth face. If this was indeed the rationale, the sisters were soon proven wrong.[82]

From Town to City

Real estate speculators were laying out new residential areas, and the city's commercial district was outgrowing the traditional confines of Main and Military plazas and Commerce Street. When Augustus Koch drew his bird's-eye map of San Antonio in 1873, the Ursuline convent was no longer isolated on the city's northern edge. The school was surrounded by a neat grid of streets, interrupted only by the irregular meanders of the San Antonio River. Imposing homes built 25 years earlier on the banks of the river were now surrounded by newer, more modest structures clustered along Second (today's Augusta), Soledad, and Acequia (today's Main) streets.[83]

By 1871 the Ursuline convent had 260 day students, 40 boarding students, and 15 teachers who instructed the girls in English, French, Spanish, and German as well as all courses required "by a polite education of young ladies."[84] The school was presided over by Mother Mary

Magdalen, who had come to teach Spanish as a young girl shortly after the school opened in 1851.[85] In 20 years she had joined the Ursuline Order, succeeded in becoming the convent's superior, and witnessed the school's growth to become a thriving educational institution. The course of instruction was impressive, including not only languages but also geography, astronomy, natural history, philosophy, mythology, mineralogy, botany, and physiology.[86] Music, drawing, and painting classes were available for an additional charge.[87] The cost of board, tuition, and laundry for

Augustus Koch's 1873 bird's-eye view of San Antonio illustrated the Ursuline convent adjacent to the meandering San Antonio River. *Courtesy of the Witte Museum, San Antonio, Texas.*

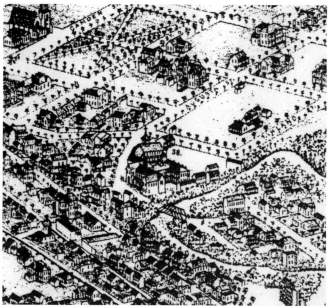

JOHN M. CAMPBELL,
ARCHITECT & BUILDER,
SAN ANTONIO, TEXAS.

Informs his numerous friends and the public that he is now prepared to execute all kinds of STONE-WORK, PLASTERING, &c. He will give particular attention to the building of CISTERNS, which he does in his *famous style.*

Feb. 8th, '66.   dly.

the school term that began the first Monday of September and extended through the middle of July was $190. When the Ursuline convent celebrated its twenty-fifth year in 1876, the school offered a challenging curriculum and enjoyed substantial enrollment.

Growth of the sisters' program both enabled and necessitated additions to the school complex. Mother Mary Magdalen signed a contract in October 1872 with local architect and builder John Campbell to construct a two-story rock building.[88] In September 1880 another new addition, by builder Henry Pauly, was "marching upward rapidly."[89] Pauly was retained again three years later to construct a two-story school building for $4,000.[90] When Augustus Koch drew his second bird's-eye view of San Antonio in 1886, the Ursuline was an impressive complex that intrigued residents and visitors alike. Sidney Lanier described the limestone buildings' dormers and lattice covered balconies, while O. Henry wrote of the sisters' evening chants wafting over the walls. The convent remained virtually unchanged until 1910.[91]

Meeting the Challenge of Public Education

Changes to the Texas constitution had provided greater funding for public education, and to stay competitive private schools such as the Ursuline Academy were forced to modernize and expand their curricula. Construction of the school building in 1883 coincided with the sisters' application to receive a state charter for the institution that they officially named the Ursuline Academy. The Ursuline, now on equal footing with its public school counterparts, awarded its first diploma to Kate Dillon in 1884.[92]

The City of San Antonio had created a free public school system as early as 1854, but it was not until 1867 that the council voted to build four schools, one of them "solely for the education of the colored children of San Antonio."[93] The school for San Antonio's African American children was built directly across the river from the Ursuline convent on Rincon Street (today's St. Mary's Street).[94] San Antonio's public schools were placed under the city's direct supervision in 1875. Then, in 1883, the same year Ursuline Academy received its state charter, the city invested $100,000 to construct its new Central High School only one block from the Ursuline on Acequia Street.[95]

The Ursuline sisters successfully expanded the academy's curricu-

Opposite top: The Ursuline sisters made additions to their convent in 1872, 1880 and 1883, the year that the school received a state charter and was officially named the Ursuline Academy. *Zintgraff Collection, The Institute of Texan Cultures.*

Opposite bottom left: The 1886 bird's-eye view depicted the town's rapid growth and the construction of a sturdy iron bridge connecting the convent to the center of the city. *Courtesy of the Witte Museum, San Antonio, Texas.*

Opposite bottom right: Local architect and builder John Campbell constructed a two-story building for the Ursulines in 1872. *San Antonio Herald.*

lum to face the challenge of public education, adding courses including bookkeeping, chemistry, and logic. By the early 1880s the school had 18 teachers, 80 boarding students from as far away as West Texas and Mexico, and a total enrollment of 250. The sisters admitted students of all religious denominations and accepted day students regardless of their ability to pay.[96]

Life within the walls of the Ursuline convent was protected and seemingly idyllic. At long tables in the refectory the girls dined on "convent stew," a concoction that varied depending on available ingredients, and on special occasions, they were treated to a small glass of sweet red wine.[97] Before their weekly baths, boarding students traipsed to the convent's attic to fetch fresh outfits from their trunks. They remembered with glee sliding down washboards before being caught and scrubbed by the sisters.[98]

Students who stayed for the summer slept outside on the open galleries and enjoyed games of croquet and swims in the river, shielded from view by the surrounding bathhouse. The students and sisters wandered past the cemetery and through the pecan and walnut trees to the far end of the property where they rested and prayed at the secluded grotto enclosed by an arbor of red roses. There were playgrounds for exercise, and a gardener to trim the flower and vegetable gardens. Remembering her days there, one student recalled, "As I think of it, it was a sanctuary." In 1887 the school was said to have "met with the unqualified endorsement of the parents and guardians who have committed children to their care."[99]

The Ursuline Order continued to prosper as it approached the golden anniversary of the sisters' arrival in San Antonio. In 1900, when Pope Leo XIII organized the Canonical Ursuline Union based in Rome, the San Antonio community affiliated itself with the central province of the United States. The academy's superior at the turn of the century, Mother Ursula Hudson, was among the representatives called to the Vatican. In later years Emily Edwards, a student at the time, remembered the excitement among the sisters and children when Mother Ursula returned from meeting the Pope. "Armed as she was with permission to step boldly into the twentieth century, a great surge of energy had followed Mother Ursula's return from Rome."[100] When Mother Ursula and the sisters did step into the twentieth century, they found a rapidly changing city outside of their convent's walls.

Opposte top: The City of San Antonio built its new Central High School one block west of the Ursuline Academy in 1883, the same year that sisters received a state charter for their school. *The Institute of Texan Cultures, courtesy of Ellie Lamb.*

Opposte bottom: Ursuline students gathered in the school's courtyard in 1874. *Ursusline Provincialate. Crystal City, Missouri.*

Above: Artist Robert Jenkins Onderdonk depicted a nun walking along the meander of the San Antonio River behind the school's washhouse and stables in his c. 1885 painting, View of the Old Ursuline Academy. *Lent anonymously.*

Right: The meander along the San Antonio River was a favorite gathering place for the sisters and their students, depicted in this "Souvenir of Our School," on September 12, 1885. *Southwest School of Art and Craft.*

Above: The Ursuline sisters, students, and priests gathered in the yard and on the balcony of the dormitory building to commemorate the 50th anniversary of the Ursuline Academy in 1901. *Ursuline Provincialate, Crystal City, Missouri.*

Left: Ursuline Academy students gathered on the school's lawn about 1900 to celebrate their graduation. *Ursuline Provincialate, Crystal City, Missouri.*

A thriving residential neighborhood surrounded the Ursuline Academy by 1910 when the sisters undertook to modernize their school. Newly landscaped grounds and changes to the 19th century priest's house, including a decorative parapet and dormer windows, are seen in this c. 1915 photograph. *Ursuline Provincialate, Crystal City, Missouri.*

The school had been founded in 1851 on the remote northern edge of a city with an estimated 3,500 residents, no other religious schools, and no public school system. Fifty years later San Antonio had 53,000 residents. When the first decade of the twentieth century ended, the city's population exceeded 96,000 residents, and there were 14 Catholic schools and a strong public school system. Ursuline Academy continued to attract students from throughout South Texas and Mexico, but the sisters understood that in order to remain competitive they needed to continually modernize and enlarge their school and educational program. Reaching beyond their walled cloister, they assumed teaching duties at St. Michael's School on the near east side to serve the city's growing Polish population and established Sacred Heart Academy on the city's west side to teach Spanish-speaking children.[101] Having expanded their educational mission, the sisters announced in March 1909 that they would spend $150,000 to enlarge, remodel, and beautify Ursuline Academy.[102]

Shaped by the Changing City

Modernization of Ursuline Academy coincided with reconstruction of San Antonio's downtown infrastructure, a project undertaken by city fathers to address increased congestion and suburban growth. By the early 1900s the school's once-isolated site was surrounded by residential neighborhoods that were gradually yielding to commercial zones. Residents could now live farther from the center of town and

Left: The Ursuline Academy and Ursuline Academy of the Sacred Heart on Prospect Hill both offered a boarding and a day school for young ladies in this 1905 advertisement. *General Directory and Blue Book of the City of San Antonio, 1905-06, page 197.*

ride streetcars or drive automobiles to work. Many chose to move to the city's new subdivisions that extended in all directions—north to the rocky ridges of Laurel Heights and Alamo Heights, south to Highland Park, east to East End, and west to Prospect Hill.[103] To ease the movement of traffic from downtown to the suburbs, streets were extended and new bridges built across the San Antonio River. Property owners with vested interests along the proposed thoroughfares argued over street alignments that would either enhance or diminish their land values. The Ursuline sisters were no exception.

During the spirited community debate over whether to extend either Navarro Street or St. Mary's Street north across the San Antonio River adjacent to the academy, the sisters favored the Navarro Street option, arguing that it would better serve the school's expansion.[104] The citizens committee convened to discuss the matter included prominent banker William C. Sullivan, a Roman Catholic who expressed the group's willingness "to be influenced largely by the wishes of the academy authorities." Not surprisingly, the Navarro Street option prevailed.[105] On May 24, 1909, the city council approved the purchase of a 55 foot by 600 foot strip of land from the Ursuline sisters for $4,000, stating that it would provide "great relief to the congested condition on Main, Soledad and Houston streets."[106] By 1910 the Navarro Street bridge had been constructed, the street extended, and Ursuline Academy had a new front door.

The Navarro Street extension created new opportunities for the Ursuline sisters. Not only did they reorient their campus and enlarge their school, they also prepared to sell two acres of the convent's land purchased by John Odin in 1840. "The Meander," as it was called, was once a contemplative and secluded retreat where the sisters and their students wandered along the river's edge. The land now bordered on the new extension of Navarro Street and was more valuable as saleable real estate. It could be subdivided and sold to help finance the academy's ambitious expansion plan. On September 23, 1909, the sisters met and voted to authorize Reverend Mother Ursula to sell "lands now or lately part of the Ursuline Academy grounds in San Antonio, Texas."[107] The property was platted as the Ursuline Addition subdivision on November 20, 1909, and Mother Ursula began to sell lots.[108]

Hoping to control development adjacent to their school, the sisters restricted the 15 lots to residential use and charged prices ranging from $2,500 to $7,500, depending on size.[109] The largest of the parcels was an irregularly shaped tract in the bend of the river that was prone to flooding and therefore apparently undesirable. William Sullivan, who had urged the city to heed the sisters' desire to extend Navarro Street, knew otherwise. On December 4, 1909, he purchased Lot 15 from Mother Ursula for $3,000 and sold it four years later to the Coliseum League, a civic group organized to promote the construction of a municipal auditorium.[110] The organization then spent almost ten years

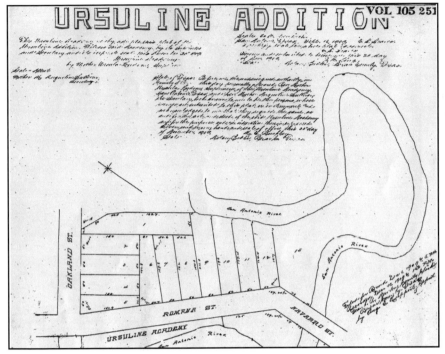

Left: The Navarro Street extension provided a new entrance to the Ursuline Academy, and the sisters took the opportunity to sell the land east of their school, dividing it into 15 lots that they called the "Ursuline Addition." *Bexar County Plat Records.*

Bottom: The extension of Navarro Street across the San Antonio River in 1909 bisected the Ursuline sisters' land, and the old river bed was subsequently filled when a straight concrete channel was constructed to control flooding. *San Antonio City Engineer's Office.*

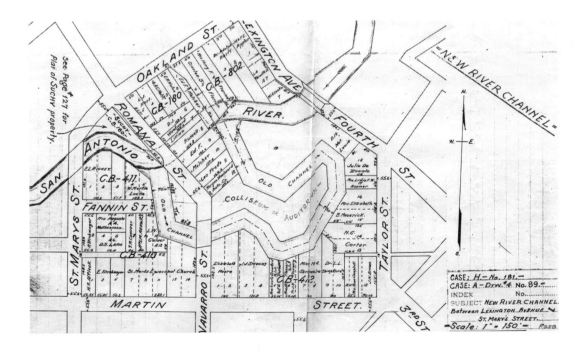

Top: Two of the Ursuline's 19th century buildings, the Angel's Hall (left) and Select School (right), were remodeled to become wings flanking the new 1910 academy building. *San Antonio* Light and Gazette.

Right: Architect F.B. Gaenslen's original design for a new three-story building at the Ursuline Academy was modified and a proposed future addition was never constructed. *San Antonio* Light and Gazette.

Bottom right: The 1910 Ursuline Academy building, entered from newly extended Navarro Street, epitomized modern Catholic education in San Antonio. *Courtesy of the Witte Museum, San Antonio, Texas.*

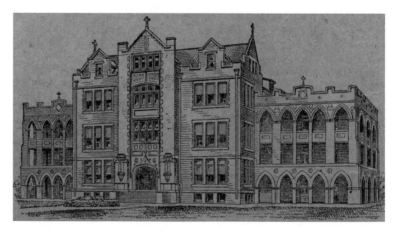

convincing city fathers and voters to fund the facility. During that decade the river meander was eliminated, a straighter channel constructed, and the old course filled to create a site for the new auditorium that opened to the public in 1926.[111]

A Twentieth Century School in a
Twentieth Century City

The same week the sisters agreed to sell the meander, they also announced construction of their new building, designed by San Antonio architect F.B. Gaenslen. The three-story academy building would be situated between the recreation building, known as "Angels' Hall," on the south and the "Select School" building on the north, and the two old buildings would be remodeled to complement the new structure in height and style. Gaenslen also proposed a second phase of work to extensively remodel the chapel and priest's house. Writing about Ursuline Academy a local journalist stated, "When completed, it will be modern in every respect and will add to the beauty of that section of the city."[112]

The new academy building was an imposing brick structure that included a recreation room, kitchens, storerooms, an auditorium, classrooms, a study hall, and private bedrooms and large dormitory rooms.[113] Arched arcades connected the new academy to the old dormitory building, and the students came to call these the "angel arches." The academy's rambling, informal landscape, a vestige of an earlier era, was transformed into a designed garden of landscaped walkways and planting beds. The old vegetable garden was terraced to the river and planted with Bermuda grass, roses, and beds of flowers; and, with the sale of the meander, the convent's Lady of Lourdes grotto was moved to the new building's courtyard.[14] When outmoded buildings, including the old chicken coop, were demolished to construct the new Navarro Street entrance, the modernization was complete, and Ursuline Academy remained largely unchanged for the next 57 years.[115]

Surrounding the refurbished Ursuline Academy was a downtown that had been drastically redesigned between 1910 and 1915. Though some residents had claimed that another bridge was not needed so close to the Navarro Street and Convent Street crossings, the growing dominance of the automobile dictated otherwise.[116] In 1914 St. Mary's

Right: The Ursuline sisters and their students meditated at the Lady of Lourdes grotto that was moved from the meander to the courtyard in 1909 when Navarro Street was extended through the property. *Ursuline Provincialate, Crystal City, Missouri.*

Street was extended across the San Antonio River, completing the transition of the academy's site from an isolated enclave to an urban oasis. For the last time the order sold land to the city in the name of progress, and in the process lost several outbuildings and, more importantly, their cemetery where 32 of their sisters were buried.[117]

During the pre-Depression boom of the 1920s, the city's skyline was completely altered by structures, including the Smith-Young Tower and the Milam Building, which rose high above the school. Two blocks east

of the Ursuline, the city's new Municipal Auditorium had opened in 1926, and immediately to the west Maverick-Clarke Lithography Company built its new store in 1929.[118]

In the midst of this construction boom and in spite of the fact that they had recently renovated their school, the sisters apparently considered future expansion or relocation. In 1926 the order purchased 20 acres north of San Antonio on Fredericksburg Road from the Balcones Heights Company for $15,000.[119]

When Congress allocated funds in the late 1920s to construct new federal buildings, San Antonio was selected for the program, and seven sites were proposed, including the old Ursuline property. An inspection team toured the sites during a visit to the city on October 8, 1929, and returned to Washington to make its recommendation.[120] Three weeks later Black Friday plunged the country into the Depression. When a site decision was finally made in 1931, postal officials announced they had decided to demolish the old federal building on Alamo Plaza, purchase adjacent land, and construct a new facility on the same location. With no immediate buyer and facing the economic reality of the Depression that gave them few sales opportunities, the sisters did not sell their Balcones Heights property until 1945.[121]

Ursuline Academy was able to maintain its stature and reputation during the years of the Depression and World War II, and in this time of national need the sisters also reached beyond their educational mis-

Above: The two-story rock building, constructed in 1872 and used today as part of the Club Giraud, dominated the school's new east entrance after the completion of St. Mary's Street. Artesian well water for the school was stored in a tower high above the grounds. *Ursuline Provincialate, Crystal City, Missouri.*

Bishop Arthur J. Drossaerts led a procession through the Ursuline courtyard during the convent's 75th anniversary celebration in 1926. *San Antonio Light Collection, The Institute of Texan Cultures.*

sion.[122] They helped the homeless and needy, fed Works Progress Administration workers who were constructing improvements along the San Antonio River, and provided food and cots for their students whose mothers worked long hours in the war effort.[123] Boarders brought ration books to assure that the school could procure sugar, meat, and other scarce supplies.[124]

There was, however, discussion in the early 1940s of closing Ursuline Academy. The school was expensive to operate, and the convent had few postulants training for religious vocations. Writing to Mother Mary Rose in New Orleans, Archbishop Robert E. Lucey defended San Antonio's Ursuline community. He had been in San Antonio only one year but already understood the school's importance to the community and admired the sisters' work. The school, he argued, was important historically and provided a sound education at a reasonable cost to the children of working mothers. Recommending against "suppression" of the local Ursuline community, Lucey concluded that the school was "a part of the historic traditions which make San Antonio loved and admired throughout the nation."[125]

Looking back, students remember the 1940s and 1950s as years

Above: The Ursuline auditorium in the 1910 academy building was the setting for school functions including this pageant, "The Court of the Holidays," in 1948. *Southwest School of Art and Craft, courtesy of Olga Litras Callins.*

Left: Ursuline students gathered about 1943 on the steps of the academy building. *Southwest School of Art and Craft, courtesy of Olga Litras Callins.*

The centennial of the Ursuline Order in San Antonio was celebrated on July 25, 1951. *Southwest School of Art and Craft.*

filled with fond memories of the rituals and traditions that defined the school. In full dress uniform they celebrated the feasts of St. Ursula and St. Angela Merici. Freshmen received the Serviam pin ("I Shall Serve"), presented to Ursuline students worldwide to remind the wearer of her responsibility to serve God, her fellow men, and herself. The younger students gathered to witness ceremonies where seniors received pins and rings that marked their final year at the school. There were religious retreats, dramatic presentations, and school dances in the auditorium, closely watched by the sisters from the balcony above.[126] Together with a strong academic curriculum, these experiences comprised an Ursuline education, defined by the sisters as "truly formative instruction, a solid education of the mind, an education of the heart and the will while neglecting no useful branch of human knowledge."[127]

Ursuline Academy emerged from the war years with record enrollment levels that in 1951 reached 500 students. That year, in the war's optimistic aftermath, the Ursuline sisters celebrated the centennial of their school with remembrance and thanksgiving. At a solemn requiem Mass they honored the deceased nuns, chaplains, students, and benefactors who had pioneered and guided the school for 100 years. The following day another Mass was celebrated to give thanks for the many blessings realized by the order since coming to San Antonio. In his centennial sermon Reverend William Lamm remarked, "San Antonio is the greatest center of Catholic education in Texas and the South. We are here this morning to rejoice with you the Ursulines to whom God in the riches of his Wisdom and Knowledge confided the task of beginning the great work of the schools . . . we have been the beneficiaries of your work and prayer."[128]

Above left: Mother Marcella walked hand in hand with her student Sandra Kay Kvistad through the Academy's Angel Arches. *San Antonio* Express.

Above: The Augusta Street entrance to the Ursuline Academy remained a picturesque and sentimental gathering place for students 100 years after the school's founding. *Ursuline Provincialate, Crystal City, Missouri.*

Notes

Full citations to the published sources, except periodicals, referenced in the following notes will be found in the Bibliography. The following abbreviations for unpublished sources are used in the notes.

BCDR Bexar County Deed Records, located in the basement of the Bexar County Courthouse, Main Plaza, San Antonio.

CAT Catholic Archives of Texas, 1600 North Congress, Austin. Many of the early documents in this collection are in French. Quotes herein are from translations and English summaries held by the archive.

CASA Archives of the Catholic Archdioceses of San Antonio, 2718 W. Woodlawn, San Antonio. Many of the early documents in this collection are in French. Quotes herein are from translations and English summaries held by the archive.

SACS San Antonio Conservation Society and, as a source, its library, located in the Anton Wulff House, 107 King William, San Antonio.

SWCC Southwest Craft Center.

SSAC Archive of the Southwest School for Art and Craft, 300 Augusta, San Antonio.

1 Roemer, 119-120. Dr. Ferdinand Roemer, a German scientist traveling in Texas, arrived in San Antonio on February 19, 1846, the day Texas became a state.

2 John Joseph Linn (1798-1885), an Irish-born merchant, established his business in New Orleans in 1822. During his travels to Mexico, Linn became interested in Texas and settled in Victoria in 1829. He built a wharf and warehouses on Lavaca Bay c. 1831, and the port became known as Linnville. Linn was a delegate to the Convention of 1836 where Texas declared its independence from Mexico and was subsequently quartermaster of the Texas Army.

3 *Dinkins,* 10. The Catholic Church also sought to restore title to its properties that had been lost in the chaos of political upheaval. Leaders of the Republic of Texas, including Sam Houston, were aware of these concerns, a fact that helped raise awareness in both political and religious circles.

4 Blanc to Timon, March 30, 1838, quoted in *Dinkins,* 13-14.

5 Until Austin was designated as the permanent capital of the republic in 1839, Houston was among the towns that served as the seat of government. Though the congress first convened in Austin in November 1839, Timon nonetheless met with these officers in Houston.

6 Timon to Blanc, January 9, 1839, quoted in *Dinkins* 15-16.

7 Shortly before his trip to Texas in December 1839, John Timon had been

appointed rector of the seminary at the Barrens and president of St. Mary's College. His appointment as prefect apostolic came only after he steadfastly refused a position as coadjutor of St. Louis. In spite of his refusal, Timon was still deemed to be an excellent candidate for the prefecture. A full discussion of this issue is found in Castaneda, 7:6-33

8 Odin Journal, July 30, 1840, CASA. Odin arrived in New Orleans on May 12, traveled briefly to Alabama, and departed for Texas on July 1. On July 12 he landed at Linnville, a port established by John Linn, the man who petitioned Bishop Anthony Blanc to send missionaries to Texas. Linnville was destroyed by Comanche Indians in a raid on August 6, 1840, less than three weeks after Odin's arrival.

9 The Council House Fight, which took place on March 19, 1840, precipitated Comanche raids, including the one that destroyed Linnville.

10 Odin to Rosati, August 27, 1840, CAT.

11 Odin to Etienne, February 7, 1842, CAT.

12 The fifth mission, San Antonio Valero (the Alamo), was leased to the United States Army as a quartermaster's depot.

13 Odin to Blanc, October 2, 1840, CAT.

14 Odin Journal, August 24, 1840, CASA. BCDR, A2:336, confirms that Odin gave Colquhoun a note for $2,200 on September 20, 1840. Colquhoun, a former San Antonian, was living at the time in New Orleans. Colquhoun had purchased the isolated site north of the town center from Erasmo Seguin, a prominent San Antonio politician and business leader. Seguin was the father of Juan N. Seguin whom John Timon had met on his trip to Texas in early 1840.

15 Odin to Timon, September 30, 1841, CAT.

16 Castaneda,7:6-33. Texas became a state in February 1846, and when the Sixth Provincial Council of Bishops met in Baltimore in April 1846, it was recommended that Texas become a diocese. On May 14, 1847, Pope Pius IX established the Diocese of Galveston and John Marie Odin became the first bishop in Texas

17 Odin to Fransoni, December 15, 1840, CAT. The Society for the Propagation of the Faith, headquartered in Lyon, France, funded Catholic missionary work. The Leopoldine Society (formally named the Leopoldinen-Stiftung) was a German organization formed to assist Catholic immigrants to America.

18 Odin to Fransoni, January 11, 1847, CAT.

19 Odin to Blanc, December 10, 1844, CAT; Odin to Society for the Propagation of the Faith [hereafter Society], May 23, 1845, CAT. When the first 60 families in Castro's colony arrived September 3, 1844, Odin lost no time laying the cornerstone for their new church on September 12, the feast day of St. Louis.

20 Odin to Fransoni, September 12, 1845, CAT.

21 Odin to Fransoni, January 11, 1847, CAT; Odin to Etienne, July 21, 1846, CAT. Claude Marie Dubuis also arrived in Galveston in January 1847 and received his orders from Odin. He was assigned to the colony near San Antonio that had been named Castroville.

22 Odin to Etienne, August 4, 1845, CAT.

23 Ibid.; Odin to Timon, August 8, 1845, CAT. Odin envisioned raising crops to supply the school on the fields adjoining the Alamo and Mission Concepción.

24 Odin to Etienne, June 23,1849, CAT. In June 1849 Odin traveled to Washington D.C. "to lay claim to the Alamo Mission." which he described as "perfectly restored."

25 "The Texas centennial of statehood and Bishop Dubuis," Southern Messenger, February 14, 1946.

26 Odin to Blanc, April 18, 1847, CAT; Odin to Society, April 9, 1847, CAT.

27 Odin to Etienne, June 23,1849, CAT. The Alamo church was not restored for worship nor was a school built on the grounds. It was not until 1857 that a second Catholic Church, St. Mary's, was completed.

28 *Everett*, 7.

29 *Everett*, 11, quoting Red, 72-73.

30 *Everett*, 10-11.

31 Odin to Society, May 14, 1849, CAT.

32 F. Giraud, as he was often called, was born François Pierre Giraud on June 1, 1818.

33 As Frenchmen and Catholics, it is not surprising that François and Theodore Giraud received commissions from Bishops Odin and Blanc, but exactly how and when they became acquainted is not known. Theodore Giraud worked for Bishop Blanc in New Orleans as early as 1848 (T. Giraud to Blanc, March 19, 1848, CASA).

34 F. Giraud to Odin, January 15, 1849, CAT.

35 F. Giraud to Odin, February 10, 1849, CAT.

36 F. Giraud to Odin, January 15, 1849, CAT.

37 *Pisé de terre*, or rammed earth construction, uses clay of low moisture content. When used in construction of a wall, the clay is packed between forms that are raised incrementally as the wall increases in height.

38 *Letters from the Ursulines*, 214. The City of San Antonio owned the town's major rock quarry, located near the headwaters of the San Antonio River (today a part of Brackenridge Park).

39 San Antonio *Light*, August 6, 1885. Poinsard's obituary states that he came to Texas with Victor Considerant in 1846. This appears to be erroneous as Considerant, a leading member of the democratic socialist movement in France, first came to the United States in 1852 and did not immigrate to stay until 1855. Considerant founded the colony of La Reunion near Dallas, and when it failed in 1859 he and his wife moved to San Antonio where he became an American citizen. While living in San Antonio, they were acquainted with their fellow Frenchmen, including Poinsard. Though BCDR, F2:434, records that Poinsard purchased property from Henri Castro on November 17, 1847, there is no record that he was a member of Castro's Colony.

40 François Guilbeau was the French consul in San Antonio. Preservation of the Guilbeau house became a cause celebre with the San Antonio Conservation Society in the early 1950s. Guilbeau has been credited with shipping wild Texas mustang grape stock to France for grafting to French vines, saving the wine industry from a deadly

infestation of philioxera. Interestingly, Jules Poinsard's obituary notes that he was appointed by the French government as commissioner of agriculture in Texas to study the same procedure credited to Guilbeau.

41 San Antonio *Texan*, January 4, 1855. A "perch" probably refers to a layer of clay. In his advertisement, Poinsard advertised other skills, including printing, sculpture (he also sold parlor statues), drafting, architecture, and "laying off of gardens." 1850 Census, 65.

42 F. Giraud to Odin, March 4, 1849, CAT.

43 F. Giraud to Odin, March 17, 1850, CASA.

44 F. Giraud to Odin, February 23, 1851, CAT.

45 Ibid.

46 Odin to Blanc, May 23, 1851, CAT. New Orleans was named an archdiocese in 1850, and Bishop Blanc was elevated to archbishop on February 16, 1851.

47 Blanc to Whom It May Concern, August 26, 1851, CAT.

48 *Letters from the Ursuline*, 291-92.

49 *Letters from the Ursuline*, 359. It is unclear if the "architect" referred to here was François Giraud or Jules Poinsard.

50 References to Ned Walshe contained in the *Letters from the Ursuline* lead to speculation that he was the brother of Sister Mary Patrick Joseph Walshe.

51 *Letters from the Ursuline*, 223.

52 Ibid., 359.

53 Anonymous undated manuscript, translated by Sister Mary Genevieve, O.S.U., SSAC. This document in French was found in the Ursuline Academy attic about 1968 by John M. Garner, who was conducting a Historic American Buildings Survey of the site.

54 *Letters from the Ursuline*, 144.

55 Ibid., 296. An ad (San Antonio *Ledger*, October 16, 1851) gives the opening date as November 1, a Saturday. The school's early records were destroyed by San Antonio's 1921 flood, and the Irish sisters' letters remain the most comprehensive account of the convent's early history.

56 Odin to Blanc, July 14, 1852, CASA.

57 *Letters from the Ursuline*, 145.

58 "The Ursulines in San Antonio," Undated typescript, CAT. The student was Kate Campbell.

59 *Letters from the Ursuline*, 353-54.

60 Ibid., 155.

61 Odin to Society, August 25, 1852, CAT.

62 Odin to Society, July 1, 1853; January 9, 1853; CAT.

63 San Antonio *Ledger*, March 17, 1853, as quoted in Sheridan, 302.

64 Dubuis to Odin, June 9, 1853, CAT. Six months later Bishop Odin sold the convent property to the Ursuline Order (BCDR L2:29, December 9, 1853).

65 James Pearson Newcomb came to San Antonio in 1847. He apprenticed at the *Western Star* and San Antonio *Ledger* before starting his own paper, the *Alamo Star*, first

published on March 25, 1854. He changed the name to the San Antonio *Herald* in April 1855. Newcomb was known for his conservative, pro-Union stance.

66 San Antonio *Herald*, September 25, 1855. The City of San Antonio established a public school system in 1854, opening a school for girls on Military Plaza and a school for boys on Alamo Plaza in existing buildings.

67 Odin to Blanc, October 10, 1853, CAT; Odin to Verdet, October 25, 1854, CAT.

68 Agreement between Schmitt and Dubuis, September 12, 1855, CAT. The structure was not plastered until September 1855.

69 Parisot and Smith,125.

70 St. Marie to Odin, May 8, 1864, CASA.

71 Parisot and Smith, 121; Johnston, 109. Some 35 years later, boarding school students from Galveston's Ursuline Academy were sent to San Antonio for refuge in the wake of the disasterous 1900 hurricane (Edwards, 49).

72 St. Marie to Odin, August 19, 1865, CASA; Parisot and Smith, 121. "Governor Madero" perhaps refers to Evaristo Madero, a politically powerful business-man with ties to San Antonio.

73 Buffard to Odin, June 8, 1866, CASA.

74 Dubuis to Odin, November 28, 1865, CASA.

75 Buffard to Odin, June 8, 1866, CASA. Francis Schmitt had also constructed the addition to the convent in 1853. At the time he undertook construction of the Ursuline dormitory, Schmitt and his brother, Joseph, were also serving as contractors for St. Mary's Catholic Church, designed by François Giraud. Though no documenta-tion has been located, it is assumed that Giraud also designed the Ursuline dormitory. The date for laying the dormitory's cornerstone is repeated in various sources, but no primary source has been located. If the cornerstone was indeed placed on September 14, 1866, the building was already nearing completion.

76 "The convent and college," San Antonio *Daily Herald*, October 11, 1866.

77 Herff, 1:76.

78 "City improvements," San Antonio *Daily Herald*, January 29, 1867.

79 "Bridge finished," San Antonio *Daily Herald*, October 11, 1866.

80 J.H. Kampmann, a prominent local builder and architect, also operated a lum-beryard. The Ursuline convent's account with Kampmann (SSAC) from January 11, 1868, through October 5, 1869, documents substantial purchases of flooring, doors and frames, windows, molding, and benches. Again, no primary source has been found to document when the chapel cornerstone was laid.

81 "Convent clock," San Antonio *Daily Herald*, April 22, 1868. Visitors entered and sat on the west side of the chapel, while the cloistered sisters were shielded from view at the north side of the chapel.

82 San Antonio *Daily Herald*, April 22, 1868. The clock was said to have been "brought from France expressly for this new chapel at something near five hundred dol-lars expense." Different sources offer varying explanations for the clock's missing north face. As the clock was erected immediately after the Civil War, some believe this to be

a reaction by the Southern Confederacy against the Northern Union. Mary Elizabeth Droste, in her research about French architecture and its influence on the Ursuline Convent (SSAC), indicates that French clocks sometimes lacked a fourth face.

83 The Worwick Tunstall house stood at the site of today's Providence High School, and the Nat Lewis house stood on Fourth Street and the river, now the site of a hotel.

84 "Education in San Antonio," San Antonio *Daily Herald*, April 30, 1871.

85 Rudicinda de la Garza, who became Sister Mary Magdalen, served four terms as superior of the Ursuline Order in San Antonio. The terms were 1869-72, 1875-81, 1884-90, and 1893-96. She died in 1897.

86 "Closing exercises of the Ursuline convent," San Antonio *Daily Herald*, July 14, 1872. By July 1872 it was reported that the school had 57 boarders and nearly 300 day students.

87 San Antonio *Weekly Herald*, September 23, 1876.

88 Though François Giraud did not die until 1877, the sisters apparently turned to John Campbell as their architect. It is possible that Giraud, who served as mayor from 1872 to 1875, was not practicing architecture at the time. The building measured 47 by 21 feet and had six doors and two windows on the first floor, seven doors and one window on the second floor, and two flues (Contract between Sr. de St. Madeline and Campbell, August 3, 1872, SSAC). The only structure fitting this description illustrated on the 1873 Augustus Koch bird's-eye view is the building on the river now incorporated into Club Giraud.

89 San Antonio *Daily Express*, September 3, 1880. This was the building later called the "priest's house."

90 San Antonio *Daily Express*, June 29, 1883. This was a freestanding building located north of the dormitory that was called the "Select School." It was remodeled and incorporated into the 1910 academy addition and was demolished in the 1967 fire.

91 Sidney Lanier, who came to San Antonio for his health in 1872, recorded his impressions of the town in a sketch titled "San Antonio de Bexar" published by William Corner in 1890. William Sydney Porter, writing under the name O.Henry, maintained an office for his publication the "Rolling Stone" in San Antonio in about 1895. He romanticized the Ursuline convent in his story, "The Enchanted Kiss.." A small, $600 addition was made in 1887, but its location has not been confirmed. "Improvements," San Antonio *Daily Express*, July 6, 1887.

92 "The best is none too good," San Antonio *Express-News Magazine*, July 22, 1951.

93 "Free schools," San Antonio *Daily Herald*, February 28, 1867; Heusinger, 26.

94 Initially called simply "Rincon School," the school in 1896 was named Riverside School, and in 1904 Frederick Douglass School. It was relocated to the city's east side in 1914.

95 Heusinger, 34, 42. The school was later named Main Avenue High School, and today its site is occupied by Fox Tech High School.

96 Children who paid full tuition were taught in the "Select School," while stu-

dents able to pay little or no tuition were taught in the "Poor School." Eventually, all of the children were taught together.

97 Edwards, 10-13.

98 Ibid., 17-19.

99 Ibid., 70; Morrison,143-44.

100 Edwards, 54.

101 The Ursuline sisters began to teach at St. Michael's School as early as 1880 and established Sacred Heart School in 1895.

102 "Ursuline Academy will spend $150,000 in improvements," San Antonio *Daily Express,* March 11, 1909.

103 Rock quarries north of the city in today's San Pedro Springs and Brackenridge parks provided building material for many San Antonio structures, including the later Ursuline convent buildings.

104 "Ursuline Academy will spend $150,000 in improvements," San Antonio *Daily Express,* March 11, 1909.

105 Ultimately, bridges were built on both Navarro and St. Mary's streets and the thoroughfares were extended at the academy's east and north perimeters.

106 San Antonio City Council Minutes, S:773-776, May 24, 1909. The city actually provided $2,000 in public funds while private subscribers, including 19 prominent businessmen and women and corporations, donated another $2,000.

107 BCDR, 316:578, September 23, 1909.

108 Bexar County Plat Book, 105:251, December 10, 1909.

109 In the next two decades, many purchasers were released from the residential deed restriction.

110 BCDR, 326:40-41, December 4, 1909; "Coliseum advocates nearing goal," San Antonio *Express,* March 16, 1913. William Sullivan helped organize the Coliseum League, and sold Lot 15 to the group for $25,000 (BCDR, 501:111-12, November 18, 1913).

111 "City designates auditorium site," San Antonio *Express,* June 1, 1920. In 1919 voters approved a bond issue that included $500,000 to purchase land and build the Municipal Auditorium.

112 "New building for Ursuline sisters costing $50,000 will be a magnificent structure," San Antonio *Light and Gazette,* September 26, 1909. The extensive remodeling of the chapel and priest's house proposed by Gaenslen was never completed. Instead, a more limited project was undertaken that added exterior detailing to give the buildings a Gothic Revival appearance.

113 "New Ursuline Academy will give another beautiful building to business section of city," San Antonio *Light and Gazette,* April 3, 1910.

114 Ibid., May 8, 1910.

115 The 1910 academy building burned on February 11, 1967.

116 "How business section will be changed when St. Mary's Street is opened," San Antonio *Express,* February 8, 1914.

117 Herff, 1:76. Remains of those disinterred from the Ursuline cemetery in 1912

were reportedly re-buried in San Fernando Cemetery #1. This process was presided over by Dr. Ferdinand Herff who, as had his grandfather before him, served as the sisters' doctor. There is no record of the reburial in the San Fernando Cemetery files.

118 The Maverick-Clarke building was purchased by Sears, Roebuck and Company, which moved its store to this location in 1937.

119 BCDR, 905:328, August 16, 1926. "Ursuline Academy is sold to Cornerstone," San Antonio *Express*, October 18, 1992.

120 "7 sites for San Antonio's new post office inspected," San Antonio *Express*, October 9, 1929.

121 "City compromises land swap terms to avoid tie-up," San Antonio *Express*, October 19, 1933; BCDR 2145:515, June 27, 1945.

122 The school, which had received its affiliation with the Texas Department of Education in 1920, was admitted to the Southern Association of Colleges and Secondary Schools in 1934.

123 Lacey, 45.

124 Lacey, 50.

125 Lucey to Mother Mary Rose, February 2, 1942, CASA.

126 Bolner to author, March 22, 2001. Clifton Bolner, a student at nearby Central Catholic High School in the 1940s, recalls attending Ursuline Academy dances and having the sisters enforce a one-foot distance between partners.

127 The Ursuline Nuns to Parents of Ursuline Girls, August 1955, SSAC.

128 Lamm, Sermon at Ursuline centennial Mass, July 25, 1951, SSAC.

SAVING *the* LANDMARKS

1952-1965

Moving North to "Green Pastures"

As the Ursuline sisters marked their centennial in San Antonio in 1951, the city was celebrating its post-war recovery with a boom reminiscent of the 1920s. San Antonio's first expressway had been completed in 1949, and by the middle 1950s pastures at the outskirts of town were transformed into tree-shaded suburbs that housed growing baby-boom families. While shoppers still flocked to downtown department stores, theaters, and restaurants, residents of newly developed neighborhoods were attracted to suburban shopping centers. An irreversible trend was shifting the city center away from the old downtown.

The Ursuline Order had postponed closing its school in the 1940s but now reexamined the situation and determined that the academy's aging buildings and downtown location were liabilities. San Antonio's demographics pointed to a successful future in the northern suburbs, where most of the residential growth was occurring. Guided by this reasoning, in 1953 the Ursulines requested archdiocesan permission to sell their downtown property, and they began negotiations to purchase a 50-acre tract that they called "Green Pastures." Mother Anita Mueller wrote to Archbishop Lucey in November 1953 about the pending purchase, and the following February, the sale was completed.[1] At this site, nine miles from their old home and far from the winding river, the sisters would build a modern school for future generations of San Antonio girls. Excited by their plan the Ursulines began to seek a buyer for their historic home.

Preserving a French Landmark

During the early years of the 1950s while the Ursuline Order was reaching its decision to move from downtown, the San Antonio Conservation Society embarked on a plan to preserve one local landmark associated with each of Texas' six flags.[2] The organization, devoted to preserving the city's historic sites, buildings, and customs, selected as its "French" landmark an imposing two-story stone house built for François Guilbeau. Guilbeau had been one of the Ursuline convent's financiers and a contemporary of François Giraud and Jules Poinsard, who had designed and built the school.[3] When the Guilbeau house was razed in 1952, the Ursuline convent became the city's most prominent remaining French landmark.[4]

In March 1953 the San Antonio Conservation Society recognized the Ursuline sisters "for preserving the old stone house built by Poinsard, a French nobleman, around 1851."[5] Perhaps the award was made with the knowledge that the sisters intended to sell their historic school. Only six months later Wanda Graham Ford announced to the Conservation Society's board of directors that the sisters' asking price for the academy was $2.5 million. Ford showed a map of the property and said that she had written to individuals and organizations that might have an interest in buying the site and keeping its buildings intact.[6]

The Ursuline Academy was treasured by Conservation Society members both as an architectural landmark and as the centerpiece of fond personal memories. Twenty years before Wanda Ford raised the specter of concern over the Ursuline's fate, society members had been honored guests at the academy. On April 26, 1934, at a gathering filled with sentimental remembrances, "the Conservation Society had the unique and happy experience of meeting at the old Ursuline Convent. On a long rock paved porch beside an enclosed garden, the hallowed atmosphere was made more significant as memories were recalled by

many members who had attended school within these very walls."[7] Isabelle Callaghan Jones, the oldest living graduate, attended, as did Florida Tunstall Sharpe, whose imposing family home stood north of the Ursuline. Essie Jones remembered the sisters washing her hair with egg and rainwater.[8] Floy Edwards Fontaine and Helen Edwards Syfan were there to recall their childhood years at the school. The occasion was described as "like a happy alumni meeting."[9]

Two decades after that gathering, real estate advertisements announced, "Must be sold, unusual opportunity to buy valuable downtown property in San Antonio, Texas."[10] The ads attracted much attention, but no buyers. Sales prospects were apparently so scarce that the

When San Antonio's most venerated French landmark, the François Guilbeau house, was demolished in 1952, the Ursuline Academy became the focus of preservation efforts by the San Antonio Conservation Society. *The Institute of Texan Cultures, courtesy of the San Antonio* Express-News..

matter was not discussed officially by the Conservation Society for almost two years. In 1955 architect O'Neil Ford, a noted historic preservation advocate and husband of Wanda Ford who had been elected the society's president, suggested that the Ursuline Academy might provide the site for "a wonderful Western Museum" directed by noted Texas writer J. Frank Dobie.[11] Over the next 15 years many other uses would be suggested and discarded until the San Antonio Conservation Society finally purchased a portion of the property and located an appropriate tenant.

In the Shadow of Progress

Mother Anita Mueller reported to the archbishop as early as December 1956, "We had made exhausting efforts to do so [sell] but everyone working on the project has failed to date." The Ursuline sis-

The Ursuline sisters made the decision to sell their property in 1953, and it was advertised "at an attractive price" and "suitable for almost any type of development."
Southwest School of Art and Craft.

MUST BE SOLD

UNUSUAL OPPORTUNITY TO BUY VALUABLE DOWNTOWN PROPERTY IN SAN ANTONIO, TEXAS

This choice property (188,982 sq. ft.—over four acres) has been occupied by the Ursuline Academy Nuns for more than 100 years. Because the Academy is moving to the suburbs, this property is available now at an attractive price. Adjoining Sears' downtown store, one edge borders on the beautiful San Antonio River for 410 ft., and the entire property has access from four streets, with a total perimeter of 1425 ft, or approximately 1015 lineal feet of frontage along four streets. Since this property is of unusually large size, right in the heart of the downtown area, as well as in the path of further commercial growth, it is suitable for almost any type of development. For detailed information contact:

The Richard Gill Company, 700 Gunter Building, San Antonio, Texas, CApitol 6-4101

ters remained committed to moving, but they struggled until 1965 to sell the downtown site. During this time they sold their suburban property in favor of a larger tract owned by a prominent Catholic family. It was on this 105-acre tract in the Colonial Hills subdivision on Vance Jackson Road that the sisters ultimately built their new school. [12] They called the site "St. Joseph's Hill."

While sales prospects were explored, Archbishop Lucey granted the order's request to borrow $700,000 to demolish the old buildings and construct its new school in north San Antonio. [13] Invoking the memory of Bishop Odin and Bishop Dubuis and their efforts to establish the Ursuline community in Texas, the sisters invited Lucey to preside at a groundbreaking ceremony for the new campus on January 27, 1957. Perhaps through divine intervention, it rained and the groundbreaking was cancelled. [14]

Sears, Roebuck and Company had become the academy's neighbor in 1937 by moving into the eight-year-old Maverick-Clarke building. In 1957 the first of two proposals by the local store to lease the Ursuline property was rejected by the company's national corporate office. [15] Mother Anita Mueller reported the disappointing news to the archbishop. "The rejection necessitates another delay in our future building program, which delay we hope will not be too long." [16] The sisters' anxiety was compounded when the long drought of the 1950s broke in April 1957 and they were awake all night mopping up water that leaked through the historic buildings' roofs to lower floors.

The first serious offer was finally received later that year from an Indianapolis consortium that proposed a $10.6 million luxury hotel on the site. [17] Though concerned that their chapel would become "a shrine for a tourist attraction," the sisters presented the plan to Archbishop Lucey who approved it on October 29, 1957. [18] Again, the plan fell through, but there was some reason for optimism. In March 1956 construction had begun on the 20-story National Bank of Commerce Building just two blocks south of the Ursuline Academy. It was the first major building constructed in downtown San Antonio in 25 years. Writing to Mother Anita Mueller about the failed hotel plan, the archbishop commented, "on the other hand, your property is now in the shadow of the National Bank of Commerce and that makes a great deal of difference." [19]

While the Ursuline's awaited the next viable offer, they continued to operate the school.[20] In the meantime Mother Marie McCloskey, who had become San Antonio prioress in 1959, developed a phased plan for the move to the new campus. The order sold over half of its Colonial Hills site in September 1959, and on the remaining 40 acres constructed a small classroom facility where the high school opened in the fall of 1961.[21] The grade school would remain at the downtown campus until the property was sold. Archbishop Lucey, trying to remain encouraging, wrote to Mother McCloskey in July 1960, "I shall pray that you will soon find a purchaser for this downtown property."[22]

Miss Emily

Seven years had elapsed since 1953 when the San Antonio Conservation Society board heard a sale price for the Ursuline Academy, and five more years would pass before the property finally sold. The Conservation Society was renowned for the tenacity and creativity of its members and, during this time, called on these attributes to sustain its resolve to preserve the historic buildings. Not incidental to their efforts was the spiritual strength gained from society founder and Ursuline alumna, Emily Edwards.

"Miss Emily," as she was called until her death at age 91, was the strong, common thread that linked the Ursuline and the San Antonio Conservation Society. She was nine years old in 1898 when, following her mother's death, she and her sisters Floy, Helen, and Lillian were sent to live as boarding students at the academy for four years.

Emily remembered her days at the academy fondly. She wrote in her memoirs of the nurturing reception the four little girls received from the sisters and the rituals and routine that defined their days. She recalled vividly the mysteries of the stone buildings and the pathways and gardens along the San Antonio River, the contrast between the cloisters' silence and the chiming of the convent bell, and the sight and smell of burning candles and oil lamps. Emily wrote of her history and literature classes with appreciation and talked of her sewing and embroidery skills. Perhaps most important, she recalled her early fascination with oil painting. Within the convent's walls, under the tutelage of her teacher Madame Louie, Emily Edwards became an artist.[23]

Opposite: Commercial development was encroaching on the old Ursuline campus, and the sisters purchased land for a new school on San Antonio's north side, convenient to the city's rapidly growing suburban neighborhoods. *Zintgraff Collection, The Institute of Texan Cultures.*

Opposite bottom: The sisters hoped that the 20-story National Bank of Commerce building, completed in 1958, would increase the marketability of their property and hasten their move to the suburbs. *Zintgraff Collection, The Institute of Texan Cultures.*

Emily Edwards and her sisters gathered in the Ursuline Academy's garden with other students and one of their teachers about 1900. Emily is seated at the left in the second row beside her sister Floy, who is holding Lillian. Helen is seated at the right of the first row. *Floy Fontaine Jordan Collection.*

Emily Edwards would come and go from San Antonio for the next 30 years as she pursued her artistic career. On one return stay in 1923, she and a group of like-minded women who loved the city's Spanish colonial missions and other landmarks banded together to form the San Antonio Conservation Society. They met at Edwards' studio, at 220 Belvin Street near the Ursuline, and strategized over plans to preserve the city's heritage.[24] Miss Emily, who was skilled at puppet making, crafted the now immortal characters that were used to convince city commissioners to preserve the San Antonio River.[25] Pursuing her avid interest in Mexican art, Edwards left San Antonio in 1926 to travel throughout Mexico.[26] Over a decade later, in 1938, she returned to Chicago, where she had studied 30 years earlier, to become director of the Hull House Art School. Finally, in 1958, she returned to San Antonio to stay and renewed her involvement in the San Antonio Conservation Society, just as preservation of the Ursuline Academy was coming to the forefront. The Ursuline property held great senti-

Emily Edwards: A Family Legacy

Emily Edwards came to attend classes at the Ursuline Academy as a nine-year-old child in 1898 and, in spirit, never left the old buildings on the San Antonio River. Though she transferred to public school, moved to Chicago, studied at the Chicago Art Institute and in Provincetown, Massachusetts, lived in Mexico, and taught at Chicago's Hull House, she always returned to San Antonio and the happy memories of this site. Miss Emily, as she was called until her death in 1980 at the age of 91, had a deep and abiding love of historic buildings generally and the old Ursuline convent in particular. She helped found the San Antonio Conservation Society and created the group's now-legendary puppet show performed for city commissioners to educate them about the importance of the city's meandering river. Miss Emily returned to San Antonio in 1958 to stay and resumed her advocacy for historic preservation. In October 1964 she authored a proposal outlining the use of the Ursuline Academy buildings as a municipal fine arts center with concerts in the chapel, studios for crafts and fine arts, and spaces for art exhibits and performances. Miss Emily's idea did not bear fruit at the time, but only one year later the Conservation Society's president accepted the keys to a portion of the Ursuline property. When the Southwest Craft Center became a tenant at the old Ursuline in early 1971, Miss Emily's vision came true, and she frequently visited the site to observe the reality of her dreams in the making. In recognition of her devotion, the Southwest Craft Center board designated May 12, 1971, Miss Emily

Edwards Day, named her an honorary member in 1974, and dedicated the original Ursuline chapel as the Emily Edwards Room in 1983. Among the many people Miss Emily inspired was her niece Floy Fontaine Jordan, who expressed her gratitude through generous gifts in her aunt's memory. Jordan shared Miss Emily's love of historic buildings and was able to assure further renovation of the Edwards Room as the Emily Edwards Gallery, publication of Miss Emily's books about the Ursuline and François Giraud, preservation of the center's archives, and a modest but important addition—women's restrooms. Like Emily Edwards, who lived to see her dream of an arts center at the old Ursuline come true, before her death in 1999 Floy Fontaine Jordan assured the perpetuation of her Aunt Emily's memories of and dreams for the Ursuline Academy.

mental and historical value for Emily Edwards, and her dedication to preserving the buildings inspired those who struggled to find the means to do so.

The Blessing of Breathing Space

The Ursulines appeared to have finally found a buyer for their property in April 1961. Dr. Daniel Gevinson, a developer from Washington, D.C., proposed construction of a 350-unit, 18-story luxury apartment complex that he called "Poinsard Square."[27]

The plan galvanized San Antonio Conservation Society members into action, and Ursuline Committee Chairman Margaret Tobin lobbied Dr. Gevinson to save the oldest of the academy buildings. At a dinner held by the society in his honor on August 9, 1961, Dr. Gevinson assured the group that the historic buildings would indeed be saved.[28]

The sisters were confident that their negotiations would result in a

Developer Daniel Gevinson, project supervisor Walter G. Lehr Jr., and construction supervisor Glynn S. Butler (left to right) gathered in 1962 to discuss Poinsard Square, an $11 million luxury apartment building proposed for the Ursuline Academy site. *The San Antonio Light Collection, The Institute of Texan Cultures.*

sale and began to make plans for a new science building and library at their suburban campus.[29] Dr. Gevinson contributed to their optimism by taking out a $4 million building permit for Poinsard Square in July 1962, but unable to secure financing he dropped his bid a year later.[30] Shortly before leaving San Antonio, he wrote to the sisters' lawyer, "Seeing the Ursuline Academy and looking at the vision of the beautiful, golden Poinsard Tower and Poinsard Folly's restoration that I saw rising on the site, with the gondolas and gondoliers sailing along the St. Mary (sic) River nearly broke my heart."[31] Both the Ursuline sisters and Conservation Society were back to square one.

In October 1964, as prospects for the Ursuline Academy's sale dimmed again, Emily Edwards authored a proposal for Conservation Society board member Mary Drought Streiber to present to Mayor Walter McAllister. She described the historical and architectural value of the buildings and outlined the society's desire for the city to purchase the academy "as a park connected with the River Development Project." The stone structures could be preserved in their entirety to serve as "a Municipal Fine Arts Center." Edwards envisioned concerts in the chapel, studios for crafts and fine arts, and spaces for art exhibits and theater and dance performances. She argued that other cities were building elaborate and expensive fine arts centers, but that San Antonio had a uniquely suitable site at the Ursuline Academy. The center would be "a meeting place for citizens of San Antonio far into the future." Offering the mayor the opportunity to leave a legacy to the city, Miss Emily concluded, "whoever can bring the blessing of adding to the breathing space around this city's center and can foster the development of the creative potentialities of our citizens will be honored forever!"[32]

Keys to the Convent

Shortly after Daniel Gevinson's plan failed, a new apartment project was proposed for the site. Archbishop Lucey remarked, "It really looks good although we Old Timers in San Antonio find it difficult to imagine that any big businessman would build a twenty-nine story apartment project in this city."[33] Alarmed by drawings in the local press, Walter Mathis, chairman of San Antonio's River Walk Advisory Commission, weighed in on the proposal. He reminded the project's designers that the commission was anxious to review their drawings and would lend its support to a plan that would "take advantage of the historic and picturesque values inherent in your site."[34]

For a full year the developers tried to formulate an elaborate deal to construct new school buildings in trade for the old academy site. At one point in the negotiations, the sisters' lawyer wrote to Mother Marie McCloskey, "like Moses of old, you may not be able to lead the way to Colonial Hills and I may not live to see the exodus of the Ursulines from Augusta Street."[35] He was almost correct.

The San Antonio Conservation Society remained closely involved in the complex negotiations that continued throughout 1964 and early 1965. Archdiocesan officials were becoming impatient, and Vice Chancellor Monsignor P.J. Murray wrote to Archbishop Lucey, "as Your Excellency has probably noticed, the Conservation Women are now involved to the point that they have been told that if they want part of the old convent preserved, they had better buy it."[36] This was indeed the society's intention.

An agreement to divide ownership between the society and develop-

When the San Antonio Conservation Society was unable to purchase the Ursuline Academy's historic clock tower and weather-vane in 1965, and to assure their preservation, Edna and Henry Dielmann (left and center) bought the artifacts in memory of his three sisters who had attended the Ursuline Academy. They are joined by San Antonio Conservation Society representative, Nelle Lee Weincek (right). *San Antonio News.*

ers was reached, renegotiated, rejected, and renegotiated again.[37] At one point the deal was scheduled to close by April 26, 1965. Shortly before she transferred to join the Ursuline sisters in Dallas, Mother Marie McCloskey made plans to finally consolidate the school at the new Vance Jackson Road location. Again she was disappointed, and in June her successor, Mother Mary Joseph Richardson, presided over the sale.

On September 1, 1965, after months of negotiations, the sale was at last finalized, and the old Ursuline had two new owners—developer Link Cowen and the San Antonio Conservation Society. Cowen intended to construct a high-rise apartment building on his property, while the Conservation Society would preserve and restore its holdings—the first academy building, the chapel and the adjoining section of the dormitory, the priest's house, and a portion of the gardens and river frontage.[38] The convent's most enduring symbols—the clock tower and weather vane—rested on the section of the dormitory owned by Cowen. To assure their preservation Edna and Henry Dielmann purchased and donated the artifacts to the Conservation Society in memory of his three sisters, who had attended the school. It was the first of many philanthropic acts that would preserve and restore the historic Ursuline Academy.[39]

The Conservation Society's patience and creativity had finally been rewarded. The group's president, Peggy Tobin, recalled the simple moment that concluded a very long and complex process. Mother Mary Joseph was loading the order's last possessions into her car when Tobin arrived to receive the keys to the society's portion of the property. "She wiped her hands on her apron and handed me a heavy, clanking ring of keys. It was a very poignant moment, the only true moment in Texas history of which I was a part."[40] The ceremonial transfer took place on October 24, 1965, at the dedication of a Texas historical marker commemorating the Ursuline Academy. After 12 years the Conservation Society finally owned a portion of the city's most prominent French landmark.[41]

Finding Tenants

The San Antonio Conservation Society had made the largest investment in its history and was now faced with securing, restoring,

San Antonio
Conservation Society
Newsletter

OCTOBER REGULAR MEETING NOTICE
THURSDAY, OCTOBER 28, 1965
10:00 A.M.

URSULINE ACADEMY
300 Augusta Street

A REPORT ON HEMISFAIR
by
James M. Gaines

Hospitality Chairman: Mrs. Edgar J. Perron

Hostesses:
Mrs. Walter Schaefer
Mrs. Leo F. Perron

Mrs. R. M. Korth
Mrs. Ernest Lee

THE
SAN ANTONIO CONSERVATION SOCIETY
requests the pleasure of your company
at the ceremony and reception
to view the historic buildings of
THE URSULINE ACADEMY
(Circa 1853 and 1863)
300 Augusta Street
Sunday, October twenty-fourth
two until six o'clock

October, 1965 — Betty Murray, Editor

The San Antonio
Conservation Society had
worked for 12 years to pre-
serve the Ursuline
Academy and celebrated
its success with a ceremo-
ny and reception on
October 24, 1965. *San
Antonio Conservation
Society.*

[71]

A five-alarm fire on February 11, 1967, destroyed the 1910 academy building together with the 19th century Select School and Angels' Hall that had been incorporated in the newer structure. *San Antonio Conservation Society.*

and occupying its portion of the Ursuline Academy. Undaunted by these responsibilities the society's leaders searched for tenants, while its members kept a watchful eye on the property, aided by a German Shepherd named Ursel. Society volunteers were known to be intrepid, but even they must have been given pause when Ursel was stolen. Unfazed, however, the women replaced Ursel with his sister Ursa.[42]

Other losses were more disturbing. One of the chapel's beautiful stained glass windows was stolen in 1972, but later recovered. More significantly, in the cold of February 11, 1967, the 1910 academy building owned by Link Cowen was destroyed in a five-alarm blaze touched off by vagrants. Worried society members watched anxiously from the roof of the nearby Sears parking garage as firefighters successfully prevented the fire from spreading to the remaining buildings.[43] The society's board of directors, grateful that the academy's nineteenth century buildings had been saved, presented a special historic preservation

award to the San Antonio Fire Department.[44]

In the fire's aftermath Link Cowen decided to sell his portion of the Ursuline property for $1,057,000, but the society was in no position to make this purchase. Their note had been reduced through donations and the sale of "Ursuline inches," one square inch of property for one dollar, but the organization's treasury was stretched thin by other commitments. The society was engaged in two battles that consumed the majority of its limited time and budget—saving historic houses at the site of the upcoming 1968 world's fair and halting construction of a highway through the city's largest park. Only when Link Cowen reduced his price to $732,500 and offered to finance half that amount for seven years did the society approve a 90-day option.[45] The option expired when financing was not secured, and the society retrenched to concentrate its initial efforts on restoring the structures it already owned.

The society secured and stabilized its buildings while searching for ways

Dear Friend:

IT HAS BEEN SAVED! *(But not paid for)*. We need YOU, your interest and support.

Come and see the beautiful old Ursuline, which is and will remain, as it has been for over 100 years, a blessing on the banks of the San Antonio River at 300 Augusta.

Please come to our "Petit Gouter", Sunday, November 21 from 2 until 5. Your contributions will be gratefully received.

We must ALL help to keep the charm we love and for which San Antonio is famous.

MRS. DON TOBIN, President
San Antonio Conservation Society

P.S. - Wonderful added attraction: a "Left Bank" art auction of the works donated by many of our finest artists.

THE URSULINE ACADEMY BUILDINGS
(Circa 1853 and 1863)

The San Antonio Conservation Society sold symbolic "Ursuline inches" for one dollar to help offset the purchase cost of the property. *Southwest School of Art and Craft.*

to use the site. Members argued unsuccessfully to include the property in the Del Alamo Urban Renewal area—in order to leverage federal preservation funds—and discussed the possibility of a housing project for the elderly with the San Antonio Housing Authority. They considered the Ursuline as an alternative site for the society's successful Night in Old San Antonio fundraiser. Finally in September 1970, five years after purchasing the property, the Conservation Society's board discussed moving its offices to the upper floor of the first academy building and using the ground floor as an arts and craft center.[46]

While the San Antonio Conservation Society was negotiating in 1965 to purchase the Ursuline site, and the deal was anything but assured, another group of women had charted an equally uncertain course when they signed the articles of incorporation for the Southwest Craft Center. Now, these two organizations, led by some of the city's strongest women volunteers, embarked on one of the most creative partnerships in San Antonio's history.

Notes

1 Mueller to Lucey, November 16, 1953, CASA; BCDR 3455:114, February 16, 1954; "Ursulines purchase $100,000 site for new million dollar junior-senior high school in San Antonio," *Southern Messenger*, February 18, 1954.

2 SACS Board Minutes, September 18, 1951, SACS. Conservation Society board member Elizabeth Graham introduced the notion of "Texas Under Six Flags," as "a plan near to the heart of all San Antonio Conservation Society members." The six flags that have flown over Texas are those of Spain, France, Mexico, the Republic of Texas, the Confederacy, and the United States.

3 The Guilbeau house stood on South Flores near the present intersection with Durango.

4 "San Antonio landmark bows to progress," San Antonio *Light*, August 17, 1952. The City of San Antonio owned the Guilbeau house and, in spite of promises to the contrary, razed the structure. Of the six buildings originally earmarked for preservation, the Spanish Governor's Palace (Spain), José Antonio Navarro House (Mexico), the Alamo (Republic of Texas), and the United States Arsenal (United States) remain standing. In addition to the Guilbeau house, the Vance house (Confederacy) was demolished.

5 "Conservation Society makes 10 citations," San Antonio *Express*, March 8, 1953. SACS Board Minutes February 26, 1953, SACS. This recognition was part of the Conservation Society's program to cite those who preserved the city's cultural and architectural heritage. The Ursuline sisters were among the society's early honorees.

6 SACS Board Minutes, August 21, 1953, SACS. This was a called board of directors meeting, implying a sense of urgency. Society president Ethel Wilson Harris suggested contacting the developers of California's historic Mission Inn, specifically "Mr. Hamilton." The Mission Inn was founded by Frank Miller, who died in 1935. Mr. Hamilton's identity is not established.

7 SACS Board Minutes, April 26, 1934, SACS.

8 Isabelle Callaghan Jones was first cousin to Bryan Callaghan, who loaned money to Father Odin to purchase the Ursuline property. She married Griff Jones of Eagle Pass in 1858.

9 SACS General Meeting Minutes, March 22, 1956, SACS. Their sister, Emily Edwards, who would play an important role in preserving the Ursuline Academy, was living in Mexico at the time. The meeting was held at the Ursuline to honor the religious builders of San Antonio. Archbishop Robert Lucey spoke about the Church's work at the San Antonio missions. A play titled *Poinsard's Folly*, written by Conservation Society member Kay Hart was also performed.

10 "Want to buy a school? Here's one up for sale," San Antonio *Express-News*, January 31, 1954.

11 SACS Board Minutes, March 24, 1955, SACS. After the Southwest Craft Center moved to the Ursuline, O'Neil Ford donated many hours of advice regard-

ing restoration of the buildings. His firm, Ford, Powell, and Carson continued to provide architectural services to the Southwest Craft Center following his death in 1982.

12 BCDR 3915:86, August 15, 1956; Mueller to Lucey, December 18, 1956, CASA. The land was purchased from Henry J. and Eleonore Lange Menger for $123,000.

13 Lucey to File, December 20, 1956, CASA. No buildings were demolished.

14 Mueller to Lucey, December 2, 1956; January 22, 1957, CASA. This letter contains a handwritten margin note that reads, "October 29, 1957. It rained that Sunday and ground was not broken. JMc."

15 Sears, Roebuck and Company first proposed to lease the property for 20 years at $50,000 a year with an option to purchase in five years at a price of $1 million. The second offer by Sears, to lease the property for $40,000 a year, came in 1958. Walker to Mueller, April 25, 1958, CASA.

16 Mueller to Lucey, April 6, 1957, CASA.

17 Leven to Lucey, October 16, 1957, CASA. The proposed deal required the sisters to contribute their land valued at $1.37 million in exchange for $850,000 in cash and stock in the hotel corporation. The active promoter was Harry R. Ray, president of Harry R. Ray Company, which developed shopping centers. Another investor was Harwood K. Smith of Dallas. The plan was promoted by the San Antonio Chamber of Commerce as well as Henry Guerra, Jr.

18 Lucey to Mueller, October 29, 1957, CASA.

19 Lucey to Mueller, April 29, 1958, CASA; "Welcome to NBC of San Antonio," commemorative opening brochure, 1958.

20 Lucey to Mueller, April [May] 10, 1958, CASA. In an apparent effort to reduce their overhead and improve the marketability of their land, the sisters received permission in May 1958 from Archbishop Lucey to demolish some of the buildings and retain the dormitory for classrooms and living quarters. In addition to maintenance issues, the sisters were faced with health and safety code enforcement that restricted use of upper floors and necessitated the remodeling of their old buildings. They did not proceed with these demolition plans.

21 BCDR 4331:382, September 21, 1959. At the time of this sale, the Colonial Hills property included an additional three and a quarter acres purchased in 1957 from the Menger family (BCDR 4057:280, August 19, 1957).

22 Lucey to McCloskey, July 5, 1960, CASA; Heck to Leven, April 7, 1960, CASA. The sisters' lawyer, Al Heck, wrote to Bishop Stephen Leven, "I seem to sense a tacit agreement among the local boys to wait until the Augusta Street property is priced at $750,000." When the property finally sold five years later, the price was $1,057,500. The sisters' real estate agent reported to Heck that "literally hundreds are trying to help the Sisters dispose of the property and build a new plant in Colonial Hills, and each day brings new proposals and plans." When the order requested a $200,000 loan from the archbishop to begin their new school, he was unconvinced of their ability to repay the loan. He refused, but gave his qualified approval to financing the $150,000 project through a conventional lender.

23 Emily Edwards published a memoir of her four years at the Ursuline Academy titled *Stones, Bells, Lighted Candles: Personal Memories of the Old Ursuline Academy in San Antonio at the Turn of the Century.* Emily Edwards continued her artistic training after she transferred to public school in 1902, studying sculpture under Pompeo Coppini in his Twohig house studio on the banks of the San Antonio River. In 1905 she moved to Chicago to live with her aunt and uncle and study at the Art Institute of Chicago. At the request of Jane Addams, Miss Emily became a teacher at Hull House. She returned to San Antonio in 1917, taught art briefly at Brackenridge High School, and moved to New York and Provincetown, Massachusetts, where she continued her artistic endeavors. Provincetown was a popular artists' colony that attracted students and teachers from throughout the country. Another San Antonian, Rena Maverick Green, also studied there.

24 The small house had been restored by Lucy Maverick. It was demolished for expressway construction in the early 1950s.

25 A full account of the "The Goose With the Golden Eggs" puppet show may be found in Fisher, *Saving*, 3-8.

26 Emily Edwards was married briefly in Mexico, studied painting with Diego Rivera, and collaborated with the photographer Manuel Alvarez Bravo. She also researched the history of Mexican murals from their origin to modern times. Edwards published *Frescoes by Diego Rivera in Cuernavaca* (1932), *Modern Mexican Frescoes* (1934), and *Painted Walls of Mexico from Prehistoric Times until Today* (1966).

27 Popp to Heck, [April 1962], CASA; "Ursuline to be site of $11 million apartment complex," San Antonio News, July 27, 1962. Daniel Gevinson paid $5,000 for an option on the property.

28 A detailed discussion of the Conservation Society's efforts to save the Ursuline Academy is found in Fisher, *Saving*, 388-396; Ann Smith, unpublished typescript, "The History of the Southwest Craft Center," SSAC.

29 McCloskey to Lucey, December 15, 1961, CASA. The sisters approached Archbishop Lucey for a $150,000 loan to build these facilities.

30 "Apartment start on Ursuline site due in 3 to 4 months," San Antonio News, July 27, 1962. The building permit for Poinsard Square was the largest in San Antonio since the $5.5 million permit for National Bank of Commerce Building.

31 Gevinson to Heck, [July 1964], CASA; Murray to Lucey, May 20, 1964, CASA. Dr. Gevinson extended his option until mid-July 1963 but was unable to meet FHA lending requirements for the project. Unrelated to his dealings with the Ursuline sisters, he was being investigated on fraud charges and was subsequently indicted, convicted, and sent to federal prison.

32 "Ursuline Academy," Vertical Files, SACS. Strieber was the granddaughter of Ethel Tunstall Drought, Ursuline alumnus, founder of the San Antonio Conservation Society, and long-time president of the San Antonio Art League. Emily Edwards' missive was evidently never delivered by Mary Strieber. A handwritten note in the margin states, "Mary did not take it to Mayor." It is not known if or how Mayor Walter McAllister intervened on the society's behalf in its negotiations with the Ursuline sisters and developers in 1964 and 1965.

33 Lucey to Heck, July 6, 1964, CASA. The plan was proposed by developer Thomas Keehn of Dallas and New York in partnership with his architect Thomas E. Stanley and another Dallas developer, Charles Aberg. Link Cowen, a builder, also became involved with the group.

34 Mathis to Reed, July 10, 1964, CASA. The River Walk Advisory Commission was established in 1962 to advise city staff and elected officials concerning applications for building permits within the river area and all matters pertaining to municipal improvements in the river bend area.

35 Heck to McCloskey, September 1, 1964; CASA. Murray to Lucey, July 21, 1964, CASA.

36 Murray to Lucey, March 4, 1965, CASA. Another expression of impatience was made by Arthur Baird, one of the real estate agents attempting to structure the deal. Al Heck wrote to Mother Marie McCloskey on July 22, 1964, (CASA) stating that he had "lectured the good ladies of the [Conservation] Society about the facts of life and asked them where they had been for the last ten years, and where their millionaire husbands were when the old Academy was put on the market, and then, when again, Dr. Gevinson lost his option." The archbishop concurred with Al Heck in a letter dated July 28, 1964. (CASA).

37 Murray to Lucey, March 4, 1965, CASA; San Antonio *Express-News*, March 6, 1965; Fisher, *Saving*, 390; Historical files, SSAC. In the first, unsuccessful agreement, the Conservation Society would have acquired 37,000 square feet of the property, including the dormitory and first academy buildings, priest's house, and 50 feet of river frontage, and Tom Keehn would receive the remainder of the site and the chapel's stained glass windows. The sisters would retain the clock tower, weathervanes, and one bell, and be paid over $1 million—$250,000 by the Conservation Society and $807,500 by Keehn ($800,000 for the land and buildings and $7,500 for the stained glass windows). Keehn's $20,000 earnest money contract was signed on March 5, 1965.

38 "Two buildings to be saved," San Antonio *Express*, March 6, 1965.

39 Though the proposed separation of the tower and weather vane from their supporting buildings may have seemed odd to some, society members might have recalled a similar action taken in its formative years. The Conservation Society's first purchase after its founding in 1924 was a door from the San José Mission granary, bought to save its decoration from souvenir collectors. The society subsequently purchased a jigsaw puzzle of land surrounding the granary, and only after complicated dealings with multiple owners was it able to consolidate the fragmented title to the property.

40 Fisher, *Saving*, 391.

41 "Ursuline keys accepted," San Antonio *Light*, October 25, 1965.

42 Ursa was described as a large black dog who was "a gypsy at heart" and liked to chase butterflies and birds. She was cared for by San Antonio Conservation Society members who had her spayed and fed her every day. One of the resident caretakers became quite fond of Ursa and was given permission to take her when he moved (San Antonio Conservation Society *Newsletter*, September 1980).

43   The author watched the fire with her mother, Elsa Buss Watson, a Conservation Society board member.

44 "Firemen to receive plaque," San Antonio *Express,* February 20, 1967.

45 Fisher, *Saving,* 393.

46 SACS Board Minutes, September 9, 1970, SACS.

INHERITORS *of a* CREATIVE LEGACY

1965-1970

San Antonio: An Inexhaustible Field for the Artist

IT was not a surprise or coincidence that women interested in the arts and historic preservation would join together in late twentieth century San Antonio to accomplish their mutual goals. In reality, architecture and artistry had been intertwined in the city for over a hundred years. After Texas became a state in 1846, trained and untrained artists alike settled in San Antonio and recorded the still-quaint and picturesque Spanish colonial town before it grew to be a city.[1] Although San Antonio was an isolated place on the frontier, it held a fascination for visitors who were intrigued by its physical setting and multicultural customs. Reflecting on the city's ability to inspire creativity, noted painter Julian Onderdonk remarked that San Antonio offered "an inexhaustible field for the artist."[2]

Inheritors of this legacy included a group of San Antonio women who organized to promote artistic causes under the banner of the Van Dyke Art Association in 1886 and the San Antonio Art League in 1912.[3] The Art League's second president was Ethel Tunstall Drought, the acknowledged leader of San Antonio's art community who was raised near the Ursuline Academy.[4] Individuals seeking to establish the city's first public museum in the 1920s logically turned to Ethel

Opposite top: The Witte Museum opened in 1926, and the San Antonio Museum Association, San Antonio Art League, and San Antonio Conservation Society joined together to mount exhibits and sponsor programming. The Museum School of Art provided local artists the opportunity to create and display their work. *Courtesy of the Witte Museum, San Antonio, Texas.*

Opposite right Harding Black first taught at the Museum School of Art and in the 1930s joined fellow ceramist, Mary Vance Green, to work with the National Youth Administration's crafts program in La Villita. In 1978 the Southwest Craft Center honored the two artists with an exhibit of their work at the La Villita gallery. *Southwest School of Art and Craft.*

Opposite left: The Museum School of Art moved to an abandoned pump house in Brackenridge Park where sculptor Gutzon Borglum had worked in the 1920s. *Courtesy of the Witte Museum, San Antonio, Texas.*

Drought for support. With her guidance the San Antonio Art League and the San Antonio Conservation Society joined with the newly formed San Antonio Museum Association to found and operate the Witte Memorial Museum. Leaders of these organizations were justifiably proud when the museum opened on October 8, 1926. It was the first, but not the last, time that art and preservation groups would join together to enrich their city.[5]

The Witte Museum soon became the public forum where artists could teach and also create, exhibit, and sell their works. Until 1926 San Antonio had lacked such a place. When the San Antonio Art League opened its Museum School of Art at the Witte in 1927, ceramists Harding Black and Rudolf Staffel were among the first teachers.[6] Organized groups of artists, including the Art Weavers Guild and the San Antonio Printmakers, also met and displayed their work at the Witte Museum. Apart from San José Mission, where both the San Antonio Printmakers and local artist Ethel Wilson Harris maintained shops, San Antonio artists had few retail outlets for their work.[7]

The Museum School of Art remained at the Witte Museum until 1939 when it moved nearby to the old water works' pump house that had been used as an artists' studio. Between 1939 and 1942 the students at the Museum School of Art studied in the building once occupied by artists of the caliber of Gutzon Borglum, Henry Lee McFee, and Boyer Gonzales.[8] The school survived the Depression, but in 1942 the San Antonio Art League announced that it would close for the duration of World War II. This announcement proved to be, in the words of Witte Museum director Ellen Quillin, a "turning point of history of art education in San Antonio."[9]

War as a Catalyst for the Arts

The future direction of art education in San Antonio was defined during the turbulent years of World War II. Local arts patron Marion McNay had converted the aviary of her Sunset Hills home into a studio and offered it as a school for servicemen and women. When the Art League announced its closure of the Museum School of Art, McNay invited the group to move its school to her property. Her proposal was accepted, and on October 15, 1942, the school re-opened as the San

Antonio Art Institute.[10] The old pump house was again vacant but was soon transformed by local artists into the Mill Race Art Studio, where servicemen came to learn lithography and other artistic techniques.

At nearby Fort Sam Houston, where returning servicemen participated in occupational therapy, Josephine Kincaid was in charge of the Red Cross Arts and Skills program. Kincaid trained volunteers to teach art to recuperating soldiers and, after the war, organized members of her group to form the Craft Guild of San Antonio.[11] The Craft Guild, in cooperation with the Witte Museum and the San Antonio Art League, began to sponsor exhibits and lectures to promote and encourage the manufacture and use of crafts and, in doing so, substantially raised the community's awareness of crafts in the post-war years.

The Coming of Age of Crafts in Texas

Craft guilds, particularly those in San Antonio and Dallas, sustained Texas artists in the late 1940s and early 1950s when organized craft programs were virtually non-existent. The guilds provided forums where artists could exhibit with a select group of their peers and have their work evaluated by renowned, visiting jurors. These exhibitions provided exposure for members' work as they struggled to gain acceptance for Texas craftsmen on both a state and national level.[12]

It was a struggle that gradually paid off. When the San Antonio Craft Guild sponsored the Texas State Ceramic and Textile Exhibit at the Witte Museum in 1953, the local press remarked "every day more and more Texans become interested in crafts. Some of them are doing outstanding work."[13] Three years later, when the Fifth Texas State Crafts Exhibit was co-sponsored by the San Antonio and Dallas craft guilds, it was noted, "This will give Texans who are interested in crafts an opportunity to see what progress is being made in the various fields of crafts, as well as giving workers an incentive to improve their techniques."[14]

The San Antonio Craft Guild gradually expanded its vision and, in 1958, broadened its exhibit from a statewide to a regional show that included the work of craftsmen from Texas, Arkansas, Louisiana, New Mexico, and Oklahoma. The exhibit program noted that the group's annual exhibits of Texas crafts had been recognized "for their consis-

Craft Guild members Margaret Kinzie, Cecilia Steinfeldt, and Rena Dubose unpacked works to be displayed in the 1958 regional craft exhibit at the Witte Museum. *San Antonio Light Collection, The Institute of Texan Cultures.*

tent high standard, each year increasing in scope and quality."[15] Though self-congratulatory, the statement was not inaccurate. The guild had indeed helped to establish a sound reputation for crafts in San Antonio and the region.[16]

In Appreciation of Handcraftsmen

At the time the San Antonio Craft Guild held its 1958 exhibit, changes were underway at the national level that would influence the future direction of crafts in San Antonio. New Yorker Aileen Osborn Webb, long acknowledged as the prevailing force in the American Craft Movement, together with her friend and neighbor Anne Morgan had established the American Craftsmen's Cooperative Council, Inc. during World War II.[17] The group's purpose was "to provide education in handcrafts and to further and stimulate public interest in and appreciation of the work of handcraftsmen."[18] In the aftermath of the war, the Craftsmen's Council sought to redouble its efforts to "be of greater service to craftsmen in America" and, in 1956, pledged "to assist existing organizations which are providing an atmosphere where profes-

Ceramic artist Mary Vance Green met with American Craftsmen's Council organizer Aileen Osborn Webb and Laguna Gloria Museum curator David Bradley (left to right) during Webb's 1960 visit to Texas. *The San Antonio Light Collection, The Institute of Texan Cultures.*

sional craftsmen can look forward to much deserved recognition."[19] The council, originally comprised of three regions—the West, Midwest, and East—was reorganized in 1960 into six regions to better serve craftsmen throughout the country. Regional meetings took the place of the national conference, and Texas joined the new South Central Region.

Shortly after the American Craftsmen's Council was reorganized, Aileen Osborn Webb came to Austin to attend the annual meeting of Texas Designer Craftsmen. Webb made a brief side-trip to San Antonio to visit old friends and see their work and remarked about the "tremendous vitality in art and art forms" that she observed.[20] Perhaps it was this vitality that led to San Antonio's selection as the site of the Craft Council's first South Central Regional Conference that met at the Witte Museum on November 5-6, 1960.[21]

The conference was held in conjunction with the San Antonio Craft Guild's second regional exhibition. The region had been expanded to include work from seven states to reflect the Craft Council's new organizational structure.[22] Although the Craft Guild, Witte Museum, and Art League had presented exhibitions consistently for many years, the 1960 show was the most ambitious to date. Chaired by veteran San Antonio artist Alice Naylor, and juried by Harold Brennan, director of the School for American Craftsmen, the exhibit drew 400 works by 140 craftsmen.[23] It was the most impressive gathering of craftsmen ever assembled in San Antonio.

To Focus on Their Creative Endeavors

Margaret Bosshardt Pace (Willson), a graduate of Newcomb College School of Art and a San Antonio artist, entered her work in the 1960 regional exhibit. Willson, an avid believer in art education, recalled, "My college had emphasized learning crafts with painting, so I was more aware of them . . . we all had to try our hand at every craft they were teaching."[24] Margaret Willson returned to San Antonio after college, married, had a family, and continued to practice her art. Like other local craftsmen, she entered her work in both the 1960 second annual regional exhibit and 1962 third annual exhibit, juried by internationally known architect and designer Alexander Girard.[25]

In 1963, one year after the third regional craft exhibit, Margaret Willson invited a group of committed artists, craftsmen, and like-minded individuals to her home to discuss the role and future of crafts in the community.[26] Among those attending the earliest meetings were active San Antonio Art League members Elizabeth (Betty) Urschel, Helen Marie Hendrie, and Nancy Negley, and artists Mary Vance Green, Janet Shook, Joan Hixon, Blanche Hellman, and Kay Maxham.

Speaking of the initial gatherings, Willson later recalled, "But that was after I had gotten the idea—probably a good year before—from the fact that there was a seven-state craft exhibit at the Witte Museum." One participant in the meetings held in 1963 and 1964 recalled them as conversational rather than organizational.[27] The common theme of the meetings was the formation of a group to enable local craftsmen to make a living from their crafts instead of from non-related jobs. Margaret Willson remembered that when she and her friend Helen Marie Hendrie traveled to Europe together in 1964 they "talked about this the whole trip." The idea continued to percolate, but faced with personal commitments Margaret Willson admitted, "I was finally discouraged and didn't keep pushing to have meetings."[28]

One day Margaret Willson received a phone call from Betty Urschel, who was enthusiastic about the concept of a group to assist craftsmen. She volunteered to organize the effort. Willson recalled, "Nothing sounded more wonderful to me, and Betty did just that."[29] Urschel, who was president of the San Antonio Art League in 1960 when the American Craft Council held its first South Central Regional Conference in San Antonio, was a seasoned organizer, active community volunteer, and dedicated supporter of the arts and crafts in San Antonio.[30]

Helen Marie Hendrie was also involved with the San Antonio Art League and would serve as its president from 1965 to 1967. She recalled, "The initial concept of the Craft Center began when Betty Urschel was president of the Art League. The Art League was behind the support of exhibiting local artists' work for sale in the Jamboree's exhibitions. Also involved was the Craft Guild—a separate group from the Art League—which had much the same idea of supporting local arts and craft people. Between the Craft Guild, the Art League, and

Prior to opening their gallery in nearby La Villita, Southwest Craft Center founders held organizational meetings at La Sirena, Bob Winn's folk art shop on the San Antonio River. *Courtesy of the City of San Antonio.*

individuals who volunteered their time and energy . . . the Craft Center had essentially begun its mission."[31]

Meetings continued during the spring of 1964 in both private homes and at La Sirena, the elegant Latin American art gallery opened in 1962 by Bob Winn.[32] Winn, who had staged many art and craft exhibits at the Witte Museum, now applied his talents to showcasing imported works in a restored downtown building overlooking the San Antonio River. The sophisticated store was ahead of its time, opening when there were only a few restaurants and virtually no retail establishments along the San Antonio River.

At those meetings the group solidified its commitment to the long-discussed craft organization. Nancy Negley, who became one of the organization's founders, remembered, "it had to be done, it was a natural when you consider what we all had been exposed to and

lived with and loved, which was all of the arts and crafts of Mexico."[33]
Finally, in June 1965, a group including Betty Urschel's son-in-law,
lawyer Jack Guenther, gathered in Negley's home to formulate articles
of incorporation and by-laws for a non-profit organization that they
called the Southwest Craft Center.[34] The founding purpose was "to provide education in handcrafts and to further and stimulate public interest in and appreciation in the work of handcrafts and the use of craft
products for the enrichment of our lives and culture."[35] The corporation's founding officers were Nancy Brown Negley, Mary Vance Green,
Betty Urschel, Bob Winn, and Joan Hixon.[36]

Nancy Negley was elected the Craft Center's first president and
ensured that the fledgling organization received a $5,000 grant in
October 1965 from her family's Brown Foundation to begin its work.[37]
This was an enormous windfall according to the group's treasurer, Edith
McAllister, who recalled that "this was when the treasurer's report sel-
dom had more than three figures."[38] Maggie [Saunders] Block remembered that when the group began to work seriously in late 1967, "The
total resources of the Craft Center were the articles of incorporation, a
Spanish colonial altar, and some New England stone rubbings."[39] Some
of the organization's meager funds were also used to pay Bob Winn for
the ongoing use of his gallery for meetings.

Treasurer Edith McAllister would become one of the Southwest
Craft Center's most valued volunteers and later serve two terms as its
president. The story of her recruitment perhaps best illustrates the
traits that sustained the organization in its early years—friendship,
trust, and mutual respect. McAllister remembered that her close friend
Betty Urschel called to report, "'We just elected you treasurer of the
Southwest Craft Center.' Well, I loved Betty and I knew she didn't do
things idly, and I said, 'Well, OK, what is the Southwest Craft Center?'"
Trusting her friend, McAllister simply accepted the invitation as a challenge.[40]

Preparing for the World's Fair

The formative period of the Southwest Craft Center—from June
1965 until May 1968—coincided with a defining time in San Antonio's
history. As early as 1958 local business leaders began to discuss pro-

Opposite: HemisFair '68, a world's fair celebrating the cultures of North and South American, opened in downtown San Antonio on April 6. One month later the Southwest Craft Center opened its gallery in La Villita near the fair site. *The Zintgraff Collection, The Institute of Texan Cultures.*

ducing a fair that would celebrate the cultures of North and South American and reshape the city's downtown and its future.[41] Planning began in earnest in 1964 for the exposition, called HemisFair '68, that was scheduled to open on April 6, 1968, on a site at the southeastern edge of downtown. This pending event focused Craft Center founders on their dual goals to offer craft classes and demonstrations and to open a shop where craftsmen could sell their objects. They reasoned that a shop with craft activities would enrich the experience of visitors to the six-month-long fair. With hardly any time to spare, Betty Urschel summoned a group to La Sirena.

Among those attending the late 1967 meeting was Helen Marie Hendrie who remembered, "around Christmas time I got a letter from Betty Urschel saying that she wanted to meet me at Bob Winn's gallery." Nancy Negley apparently did the same thing with Maggie Block, and the stage was set. Hendrie later recalled with astonishment, "Then Betty and Nancy got the two of us together and told us that they wanted an art gallery opened in La Villita by May 6!" Maggie Block reminisced, "they told us about this great idea, and by the time we left the meeting, little did we know that they were going to take care of the rest of our lives."[42]

The timing was propitious. Helen Marie Hendrie had recently completed her term as president of the San Antonio Art League, and Maggie Block had just finished her term as president of the Symphony League. Block had returned to San Antonio in 1958, following the death of her first husband, and immediately became involved with the arts. She appreciated the creative process and understood the dilemma of artists who lacked the means to exhibit and sell their work.

Following the meeting at La Sirena, Hendrie and Block gathered their thoughts, combined their organizational abilities, and within six months accomplished their assigned task. In the process Block was elected the Southwest Craft Center's president in 1968, a position she would hold three times. Helen Marie Hendrie, who succeeded Block as president in 1969-70, was elected vice president.[43] Block and Hendrie became the nuts and bolts of the organization from the time they began to plan the opening of the gallery. Maggie Block recalled, "It was a full-time job—we took satchels of work home every night!"[44] Most of all, she remembered the commitment of the founding members to accom-

plish something new. Together they would fill a void and provide artists working in a broad range of media an inclusive setting in which they could earn a living.

A Home in *La Villita*, San Antonio's Little Village

The site of HemisFair '68 was within close walking distance of two of the city's important historic attractions—the San Antonio River Walk and La Villita. The unique walkway and improvements that characterize the San Antonio River Walk today had been completed by the Works Progress Administration scarcely 20 years before Craft Center organizers first met in 1963.[45] While WPA workers transformed the river, National Youth Administration laborers restored nearby La Villita, San Antonio's oldest remaining neighborhood, which had fallen into ruins. The city's mayor, Maury Maverick, envisioned this collection of houses overlooking the San Antonio River as an arts and crafts village where artisans would demonstrate and sell their work.

By the early 1960s the river was lush and tranquil but had attracted little commercial development. Likewise, La Villita was charming and had lived up to Mayor Maverick's expectations in its early years, but by the 1960s the city was struggling to sustain the arts and crafts village.[46] The only vestiges of Maverick's dream were a few studios and galleries maintained by artists and puppet shows that were a regular weekend feature for children.

Seeking to breathe life into the River Walk, the Chamber of Commerce created a Tourist Attractions Committee and, in 1961, commissioned a study of the area.[47] Local preservationists and designers reacted with alarm to the completed study that recommended a gaudy, commercialized approach to river revitalization. The Chamber of Commerce then invited the San Antonio Chapter of the American Institute of Architects to complete a master plan. The group, led by architect Cyrus Wagner, dubbed its proposal the Paseo del Rio San Antonio and stated, "The magnitude of the development is limited only by imagination."[48]

Margaret Willson was studying architecture at San Antonio College when the Paseo del Rio study was released in April 1963. She remembered, "At the time the river wasn't used very much, and they

Above: San Antonio's oldest remaining neighborhood, La Villita, was restored by the National Youth Administration in 1939-1941 to fulfill Mayor Maury Maverick's dream of an arts and crafts village in the heart of the city. Southwest Craft Center founders located their first gallery in one of La Villita's 19th century buildings. *Texas Writers Project.*

Left: The Paseo del Rio plan to revitalize the San Antonio River envisioned buildings where craftsmen would create and market their works. This dream was ultimately realized not on the river, but at the Southwest Craft Center in nearby La Villita. *Courtesy of the City of San Antonio.*

were going to turn the buildings around and make the river active."⁴⁹ Willson was already pondering how to make people more aware of crafts and became intrigued with accomplishing that goal in a renovated building on the San Antonio River. She chose a building and asked architect Allison Peery to "make a rough diagrammatic plan of how we could use it for crafts . . . the idea was that anybody who wanted to (could) learn crafts with an apprentice, with an existing craftsman." Willson recalled that one of her teachers, architect Emil Golla, heard her idea and remarked, "Yes, a craft activity, a craft center, would be a really wonderful thing to have on the river!" Though Willson did not succeed in purchasing the building, the thought of a riverside location had been planted.⁵⁰

The Southwest Craft Center had virtually no financial resources for Maggie Block and Helen Marie Hendrie to draw on as they weighed their options for the new gallery. They looked for space that was affordable, available, and located near the San Antonio River and the HemisFair site. The city, as it happened, needed tenants for La Villita. It was a perfect match. The house where La Villita manager Hamilton Magruder had lived for over 20 years before retiring in 1964 was vacant when Craft Center representatives went calling on city fathers.⁵¹ Among Craft Center members presenting their case to the mayor was Edith McAllister, Mayor Walter McAllister's daughter-in-law. She recalled, "I said, 'Dad, we can start a little store down there,' and he just turned around to whoever was sitting there and he said something about it, and that was all there was to it."⁵² Months of planning culminated in an uncomplicated decision, and the Southwest Craft Center at last had a home.

A Dream Come True

"Dear Friend of the Arts—At last!—the dream of a Southwest Craft Center is coming true!" The letter, signed by President Maggie Block and Vice President Helen Marie Hendrie, invited supporters to join in making the Craft Center a reality in time for HemisFair. They described the center's "charming" new home and "shop," craftsmen at work, sales of handcrafted items by over 50 craftsmen, and openings to honor exhibitors. Craftsmen and active members were invited to join

Left: The Southwest Craft Center located its first gallery at 420 Villita Street in 1968 and maintained a gallery there until 1985. *Southwest School of Art and Craft.*

Below: Announcements for the May 8, 1968, opening of the Southwest Craft Center were mailed by Ann Thomas, who became renowned for processing prodigious amounts of mail and was later elected the organization's president. *Southwest School of Art and Craft.*

Below left: A simple invitation announced the opening of the Southwest Craft Center. *Southwest School of Art and Craft.*

You are invited to the opening of - - - - -

The Southwest Craft Center

420 Villita Street

Wednesday, May 8   *3 to 5*

Hours:
9 - 5 Mon. - Sat.   12 - 8 Sunday

Thank you for helping to make the Southwest Craft Center a reality

at levels beginning at $5, and soon Membership Chairman Ann Thomas was signing up the group's first members.[53] Like others who assisted with simple tasks in those early days, Thomas had no way of knowing the extent of her future commitment. She became revered for her organizational skills and ability to process prodigious amounts of mail, and although Thomas later served as president she was always happy to undertake these basic tasks.

To fill the new gallery with objects, Crafts Coordinator Sally Simons sent letters to some 250 artists recommended by the American Craft Guild in the seven-state region and placed notices in the guild's publications.[54] The response was described as a "deluge," and Betty Urschel's house was filled to overflowing with works to be juried.[55] In addition to the gallery, programming during the six-month run of HemisFair was key to the Craft Center's plan. Weaver Blanche Hellman took charge of locating "craftsmen in action" to demonstrate their techniques at both the Craft Center's gallery and the Women's Pavilion at the world's fair.

Meanwhile, the Villita Street house was being converted to a gallery. Margaret Willson was working at the time with architect Robert Harris, and he helped her develop plans for the house.[56] Board member and artist Virgil Hagy, who later exhibited his work in the gallery, assisted Willson as her co-chairman. Stevie Tucker, in charge of the garden and gallery displays, planned the arrangement and decoration of the shop, assisted by artist Maggie Lang and Nancy Negley, who provided plants for the patio.[57] Local businesses, notably Frost Brothers and Joske's, made donations, including display cases and air conditioners. Perhaps most important, the stores contributed the time of their most creative staff members, Frost Brothers' Lessi Ellen Culmer and Joske's Caroline Shelton. The gallery was, in all respects, a collaborative work in progress until the day it opened.

The Mayan symbol suggested by Bob Winn as an insignia for the Southwest Craft Center was apt—a pair of busy hands. The hands evoked the creative process of both the Craft Center's artists and its volunteers. When all was said and done, the group had located, leased, and renovated a gallery space, solicited and juried artists' works to fill it, and opened to the public in less than six months. On May 8, 1968, while artists Ishmael Soto and Tracy Dotson demonstrated pottery making on the patio, the center's board members and supporters greet-

ed visitors and sold works by 68 artists that were displayed in their new gallery. The opening was an exciting milestone for an organization whose future would be shaped by the boundless energy and imagination of its members.

The opening of the Craft Center gallery was followed by a summer of ambitious programming that revealed the scope of the founders' vision and set the course for the organization's future. All summer, seven days a week, two shifts of volunteers assisted gallery managers Jean Schoenig and Faleta Myers as they sold art works to visitors from throughout the nation and the world. The group mounted exhibitions and held demonstrations by the area's leading craftsmen, including ceramists Nancy Pawel, Mary Green, Joan Hixon, and Bertie Smith; weavers Kay Maxham and Blanche Hellman; and fiber artist Wilanna Bristow. In the following months visitors viewed the work of other outstanding local artists, including Bruce Duderstadt's brilliantly colored hooked rugs and Margaret Putnam's dramatic oil paintings.

While in the midst of the HemisFair frenzy, Craft Center volunteers also began to raise funds and market their new organization at the center's formal opening event on August 21, 1968. Those attending "Champagne Under the Stars" enjoyed a haute couture fashion show

Above left: Southwest Craft Center members mounted exhibits and arranged demonstrations by artists throughout the run of HemisFair '68. Volunteers included (from left to right) Betty Urschel, Helen Marie Hendrie, Lucia Chen, and Sally Simon. *Southwest School of Art and Craft.*

Above right: Among the artists participating in the Southwest Craft Center's early program in La Villita was ceramicist Tracy Dotson (left). *Southwest School of Art and Craft, courtesy of Maggie Block.*

Helen Marie Hendrie and Margaret Pace Willson prepared for the Southwest Craft Center's first fundraiser, "Champagne Under the Stars," held in August 1968. The center's logo designed by Bob Winn, a Mayan symbol depicting busy hands, is seen in the background. *San Antonio* Express-News.

produced by Joske's department store, participated in a benefit auction of French designs, and dined on a French-inspired menu. Watercolor artist and Joske's designer Caroline Shelton, who in future years would donate many of her works to benefit the Craft Center, assisted party chairmen Rena Dubose, Gloria Galt, and Jacquelyn Ramsdell in creating an aura of France in the Spanish village of La Villita. As the evening ended, it seemed obvious that a new standard for local fundraising events had been set. Unbeknownst to the volunteers staging the event in the heat of that summer, the gala would become an annual event that through the years would involve countless volunteers and raise hundreds of thousands of dollars for the Southwest Craft Center.[58]

Southwest Craft Center members became, of necessity, masters of creative marketing techniques. They had located their gallery in close proximity to both the sites of HemisFair '68 and of San Antonio's new convention center. After the fair closed in October 1968, conventioneers came to San Antonio in growing numbers. Board member Kitty

From Haute Couture to Homemade Pickles

"Champagne Under the Stars" set the Southwest Craft Center on a fundraising course that has helped to fund its facilities and programs since 1968. The Craft Center was frequently assisted in its early years by San Antonio's leading department stores, Joske's of Texas and Frost Brothers. At a time when local ownership and management encouraged more direct community involvement, these stores designed and distributed advertisements and mailings, mounted fashion shows, donated prizes, and hosted in-store events. Craft Center volunteers still marvel at the French designer who flew to San Antonio with his models to stage a fashion show in the Ursuline courtyard. The events were as diverse as they were numerous and ranged from the elaborate to the simple—the popular Wine Harvest Festival, Fiesta River Parade parties, art auctions, Christmas bazaars, concerts, and flea markets. There were trips up the Mississippi and down to Mexico. Themed annual galas grew in size and scope to include live and silent auctions and corporate tables that introduced an increasing number of San Antonians to the Craft Center. Members of the Club Giraud contributed annually to support the Craft Center. Among all of these creative fundraising techniques that ranged from casual to elegant, volunteers still recall with greatest amusement the Pickle Project of 1977. When member Naomi Russell was given a truckload of cucumbers and onions from another member's nearby farm, volunteers went to work and produced an enormous quantity of pickles. Though scalded by boiling jars and steeped in the smell of vinegar, the volunteers earned a few more dollars, and the Pickle Project became renowned as the most unusual fundraising scheme in Southwest Craft Center history.

Hancock announced in November 1969 that fliers about the Craft Center and its Christmas bazaar would be distributed to River Walk businesses as well as to 2,700 bankers attending the Mid-Continent Trust Conference.[59] The following month, when the Texas Cattle Raisers' Association Convention coincided with an exhibition of the work of Houston jewelry artist Velma Dozier, Nancy Negley suggested a "for men only" opening preview. Such ideas were ahead of their time in San Antonio and set the fledgling group apart from other community organizations.

Saturday Morning Discovery

Southwest Craft Center organizers clearly recognized that hard work and fundraising were required to achieve their goals. Although the group sometimes struggled and their gains were often modest, from the outset they were successful. "Champagne Under the Stars" raised $1,500 that was used as seed money for the center's first children's programming. Inspired by Jearnine Wagner, director of Trinity University's creative educational program "Learning About Learning," and assisted by Alice Hundere, an art instructor in the San Antonio Independent School District, the Craft Center piloted a Saturday morning program for young people. From February until April 1969, Hundere and her colleagues, including Martha Fenstermaker, began working with inner-city school children and teachers from the San Antonio Independent School District each Saturday at a historic building on Eighth Street loaned by local philanthropist Margaret "Mag" Tobin.[60] The program, known informally to its organizers as the "Big Craft Deal," was an outgrowth of the school district's Unlimited Potential Teacher Resource Center, a student-teacher laboratory that targeted at-risk junior high school students.[61] The Big Craft Deal brought together teachers, students, and craftsmen, all selected by Unlimited Potential and the Craft Center for their interest in arts and crafts. When the Big Craft Deal ended and was judged successful in April 1969, organizers applied for funds through the San Antonio Independent School District to finance the program for a full year. Funding was secured, and Alice Hundere, Martha Fenstermaker, and Mary Green became paid supervisors for the program that they officially named Saturday Morning Discovery.[62]

Southwest Craft Center organizers then searched for a place closer to their gallery to locate Saturday Morning Discovery. As before, they approached the city and, on November 1, 1969, rented La Casita, a small, nineteenth century house one block from the gallery on Villita Street.[63] Once more volunteers did not hesitate to take up their hammers and to solicit furnishings and equipment from supporters. When the Saturday Morning Discovery program opened in the heart of Maury Maverick's craft village, it was chaired by Mary Vance Green, who had worked with the National Youth Administration to restore La

Every Saturday Morning a Small Miracle Happens!

Alice Hundere and Martha Fenstermaker, both crafts-men and teachers with the San Antonio Independent School District, had only $175 and the cooperation of Southwest Craft Center artists and volunteers on February 1, 1969, the day they opened the doors to an experimental arts project they called the "Big Craft Deal." Hundere and Fenstermaker purchased supplies through the school district's Unlimited Potential project and procured donated space from Margaret Tobin in an old house on Eighth Street, north of downtown. When students from the school district arrived with their teachers to participate in this learning experiment, they were welcomed by some of San Antonio's finest craftsmen, including Mary Vance Green, Kay Maxham, Joyce Treut, and Virgil Hagy. Already involved in the Craft Center's new La Villita gallery, these artists volunteered their time for this first eight-week program that introduced many inner-city children to the joys of paints, dyes, and clay. Soon other craftsmen and teachers, including Joe Cunningham and Sarah Newman, and the district's fine arts coordinator, Lisa Kefauver, were working with students each Saturday morning. In its second year the Big

Craft Deal moved to La Casita, the La Villita house rented by the Craft Center for its educational programs, and by the third year the project found its permanent home at the old Ursuline Academy. Amused observers watched fledgling artists gather in the chapel, then scatter to nooks and crannies in the priest's house, garden, and dormitory to learn ceramics, batik, fiber arts, and silkscreening. It was often hard to distinguish the teachers from the learners—and that was the point. The program was expanded to include other locations and became officially known as Saturday Morning Discovery. When the San Antonio Independent School District lost federal grant funding for the program in 1971, Saturday Morning Discovery was sustained by committed volunteers until the Craft Center secured grants from the National Endowment for the Arts and other public and private sources. The San Antonio Independent School District's $175 investment reaped an enormous return as Saturday Morning Discovery expanded beyond its founders' dreams. As the center grew in size and scope, Saturday Morning Discovery became the keystone of its evolving Young Artist Programs that now also include the Teacher Training Initiative, Summer Art Camp, and the Mobile Arts Program, serving approximately 10,000 children at sites throughout the community. It is, as they wrote in 1971, "a small miracle."

Villita 30 years earlier.[64] The program thrived in its new location, and Helen Marie Hendrie, observing the fledgling craftsmen at their weaving, batik, ceramics, and woodworking, marveled, "It is a learning thing, they are learning every minute they are in the workshop. It is amazing what they can do."[65]

The Southwest Craft Center began to hold children's art classes in 1969 at the La Villita house known as La Casita. *Southwest School of Art and Craft, courtesy of Maggie Block.*

A New Adventure in Handcraftsmanship

At the end of its first year, the Craft Center gallery had grossed over $20,000 and had returned $16,000 to craftsmen. After all income and expenses had been balanced, the organization had about $580 in the bank.[66] Volunteers from among the center's 260 members had successfully raised money, stocked, staffed, and publicized the gallery and had launched a crafts program for children. With energy to spare, they turned to the education of adults.

In early 1970 the Southwest Craft Center announced "a unique opportunity for students to share in a new adventure in handcraftsmanship offered for the first time in our area." Participants in the Southwest Craft Center Workshop were not required to have prior artistic training, though classes were also promoted as stimulating and rewarding to the experienced craftsman. Rather than formal technique the program placed a priority on imagination, insight, and individual awareness "for the student to discover and develop creative sensitivity through the medium of handcrafts." The announcement attracted 80 students to classes in ceramic sculpture, enameling, stitching, hooking, weaving, macramé, metal jewelry casting, and batik. Students were required to join the Craft Center for $5 and pay $20 to register for

classes taught by "ten noted craftsmen," who were paid $50 for four, three-hour sessions.[67] The first classes, held from March 1 to April 11, were supervised by gallery manager Jean Schoenig, who kept the records and had to shuttle back and forth between the gallery and La Casita. Maggie Block described the scene, "batik dripped on the potters, wool got into the jewelry equipment, and jewelry dust flew in all directions."[68] When the session was completed, the 80 students had completed this "new adventure," and the grateful board, perhaps happy to have weathered the experience, celebrated with a party. The invitation from Helen Marie Hendrie announced that the occasion honored "our brave and wonderful first faculty and our talented eighty students."[69] Her emphasis on "first" clearly indicated that the Craft Center was in business for the long run.

Weaver Blanche Hellman was an active member of the Craft Guild and helped organize the Southwest Craft Center's La Villita gallery and classes in 1968. Hellman died shortly after the center moved to the Ursuline Academy, and the school's first memorial fund for scholarships was established in her memory. *San Antonio* Light

Opposite: Following the success of its programming for children, the Southwest Craft Center held its first adult classes in Spring 1970. Among the teachers participating in these classes was Linda Pace (standing, center). *San Antonio Conservation Society.*

"The Brave and Wonderful First Faculty"

The group described by Southwest Craft Center president Helen Marie Hendrie as "our brave and wonderful first faculty" and in press releases as "ten noted craftsmen" included some of San Antonio's most respected and experienced artists, many of them veteran members of the Craft Guild of San Antonio. Teaching ceramic sculpture was Mary Vance Green, who had supervised the National Youth Administration's craft program in La Villita 30 years earlier. The city's most respected weavers, Blanche Hellman and Kay Maxham, were longtime Craft Guild members as was ceramist Joyce Treut. Hagar Celmins, a Finnish weaver, taught the traditional method of Rya rugs, and Bruce Duderstadt demonstrated the techniques and designs inherent in his fine hooked rugs and wall hangings. Martha Mood, widely known as a master of embroidery and appliqué, worked with students in the design and fabrication of individual works. Patsy Light and Gene and Linda Menger demonstrated the technique and design of the popular art of tie-dyeing, and students of jewelry learned lost wax casting and stone setting from Jane Welch and enameling from

Terry Gallagher. As the classes grew in popularity, the ten craftsmen were joined by ceramists Nancy Pawel and Dominic Greco, batik artist Josie Neal, costume artists Jane Keller and Douglas Burnham, and jewelers Margaret Pace Willson and her daughter Linda Pace. Instructors who vied for space in the small La Casita building and its patios recall the scene as chaotic and the facilities as primitive, but do so with wonder and nostalgia for the modest beginnings of the program that later surpassed all expectations.

Notes

1 Among these artists were W.G.M. Samuel, whose naïve paintings depicted Main Plaza in 1849, and Theodore Gentilz and Hermann Lungkwitz, whose works were far more precise and realistic.

2 Curtis, 225-26.

3 "The Van Dyke Art Club," San Antonio *Daily Express*, October 3, 1886; Woolford and Quillin, 127. The Van Dyke Art Association is thought to have been the first formal art group in Texas. Its goal to promote interest in art and to found a permanent art school was not realized, but local women and men exhibited their works in association-sponsored exhibits. Other leading citizens organized the State Art School that also held exhibits of student work. ("The State Art School," San Antonio *Daily Express*, March 4, 1890)

4 Ethel Tunstall Drought's childhood home stood three blocks north of the Ursuline at 418 Oakland Street (today North St. Mary's Street). After their marriage in 1885, Ethel and H.P. Drought built a small house at 323 Oakland and, in 1901, constructed the imposing house that still stands at 1215 North St. Mary's Street (formerly 529 Oakland) on the grounds of Providence High School. Ethel Drought served as president of the San Antonio Art League from 1912 through 1938. The Art League was established to collect and exhibit American and European paintings. Drought's country home, Droughtfels, became an informal studio and salon where artists regularly gathered to paint and discuss their work. Ethel Tunstall Drought also attended the first meeting of the San Antonio Conservation Society and contributed financially to preserving the city's landmarks, including San José Mission.

5 Ethel Drought convinced Mayor John Tobin to add a second story to the new museum where the San Antonio Art League's permanent collection would be exhibited. In the new museum the Art League was responsible for art exhibits, the San Antonio Conservation Society was in charge of history exhibits, and the San Antonio Museum Association mounted natural history displays. A fourth organization, the Scientific Society, declined the mayor's invitation to move to the museum.

6 Woolford and Quillin, 120. Initially, instructors were hired with funds from the San Antonio public school budget, but when this support was withdrawn because of the Depression Ellen Schulz Quillin offset the museum's losses by charging children ten cents a lesson. (Ellen Schulz married Roy Quillin in 1927.) Both Harding Black and Rudolf Staffel became renowned for their ceramic techniques—Black for his fine glazes and Staffel for his work in porcelain. Staffel was honored by the Southwest School of Art and Craft in 2000.

7 "History of the San Antonio Printmakers," undated typescript, Vertical Files, Witte Museum. Renowned artisans, including Mary Meigs Atwater, the "dean of American weavers," and Berta Frey conducted workshops at the Witte Museum, and local weaver, Jean (Mrs. Walter C.) Griffith, formed the Art Weavers Guild in 1936. San Antonio Printmakers was founded in 1937. The group was originally named the

Mary Bonner Graphic Arts Club in honor of the famed local printmaker. In deference to objections from Bonner's family, the group changed its name. Members of San Antonio Printmakers worked at the Witte Museum under a barter system devised by Ellen Quillin—free space for prints donated to the museum's collection. To expand its audience the club rented space at San José Mission, where artist Ethel Wilson Harris maintained her San José Pottery studio.

8 The pump house was built about 1885 by George W. Brackenridge as part of his privately owned San Antonio Water Works. The building had been abandoned when Gutzon Borglum arrived in San Antonio in 1924 and rented it as his studio to design the Trail Drivers monument. Funds to execute the monument were not raised, but the model was cast in bronze and mounted in front of Pioneer Hall adjacent to the Witte Museum in Brackenridge Park. When Borglum left San Antonio permanently for California in 1937, he gave his keys to museum director Ellen Quillin. The studio was used by artists Henry Lee McFee and Boyer Gonzales until 1939, when the Museum School of Art moved there.

9 Woolford and Quillin, 121-22.

10 Ibid., 123. Marion McNay moved to San Antonio in 1926, the same year that the Witte Museum opened. McNay was a graduate of the Art Institute of Chicago and remained devoted to art for her entire life. In San Antonio she became an arts patron, served on the board of the Witte Museum, and amassed an impressive collection. McNay built a large house north of San Antonio in Sunset Hills, and following her death in 1950 it was converted to a museum bearing her name. For a full discussion of Marion McNay's life, see Lois Wood Burkhalter's *Marion Koogler McNay: A Biography, 1883-1950.*

11 Craft Guild of San Antonio *Yearbook*, 1964, Vertical Files, Witte Museum.

12 Paul Hatgil, videotape interview with William Daley, September 18, 1995, courtesy of the artist.

13 "Texas crafts on display," *San Antonio Express*, November 16, 1953; "San Antonio Craft Guild sponsoring the Texas State Ceramic and Textile Exhibit at Witte," October 25, 1953. The 1953 statewide craft show was mounted by Robert K. Winn, a longtime devotee of the arts and crafts in San Antonio. Winn went to work at the Witte Museum in 1947 and also served as faculty chairman of the San Antonio Art Institute from 1953 to 1958. In 1965, he helped to organize the Southwest Craft Center.

14 "Program," Fifth Texas State Crafts Exhibit, Vertical Files, Witte Museum. The show's 75 exhibitors were juried by Katherine Choy, chairman of Newcomb College's renowned ceramics program). The Craft Guild of Dallas was founded in 1948, and this was its Eighth Annual Texas Crafts Exhibition. The organization's history, "The Craft Guild of Dallas: The First Thirty Years," by Esther and John Houseman (World Wide Web http://www.craftguildofdallas.com accessed October 29, 2000) notes that "this plan did not meet all expectations the first year and was not continued."; "Craft exhibition set here November 4," *San Antonio Express*, October 28, 1956.

15 "Program," First Regional Crafts Exhibit, November 2-23, 1958, Vertical Files, Witte Museum.

16 The group's 1959 exhibit was juried by Stirling Dickinson, director of the Instituto Allende in San Miguel de Allende, Mexico, together with Bob Winn's former art teacher, Lessi Ellen Woolridge Culmer, advertising director of Frost Brothers in San Antonio. A third juror was Taylor Robinson, American Institute of Designers, Dallas. The exhibit was designed and installed by Winn, and leading prize winners included Paul Hatgil and weaver Alice Kagawa Parrott, then living in Santa Fe. In 2001 Alice Kagawa Parrott still lives and works in Hawaii and Paul Hatgil, professor emeritus at the University of Texas at Austin, continues to work in Austin.

17 Aileen Osborn was married to Vanderbilt Webb, grandson of railroad magnate William H. Vanderbilt.

18 "American Craft Council, 1943-1993: A Chronology." (*Craft Horizons*, August/September 1993, 137-44). The American Craftsmen's Cooperative Council, founded by Aileen Osborn Webb and Anne Morgan in 1942, and their American Craftsmen's Educational Council, Inc., established in 1943, resulted from the merger of the two women's previous organizations. Aileen Osborn Webb had formed Putnam County Products, a marketing group for handmade goods, in 1929, and in 1939 Anne Morgan formed the American Handcraft Council. Also in 1939 Webb continued her work to expand urban markets for rural craftsmen by joining with other craft groups to form the Handcraft Cooperative League of America. From this affiliation grew America House, a retail outlet for handcrafts, and the magazine that became known as *Craft Horizons*.

19 "American Craft Council, 1943-1993: A Chronology."

20 "Mainstay of American home: Crafts in rebound," *San Antonio Light*, March 9, 1960.

21 Texas was represented by San Antonio craftsman and collector Bob Winn.

22 In previous years the exhibit included work from five states.

23 Aileen Osborn Webb, American Craftsmen Council President David Campbell, and Vice President John Sowall all attended the meeting. Local artist and educator Amy Freeman Lee welcomed participants, and Donald B. Goodall, chairman of the University of Texas Art Department, presented the keynote address.

24 Margaret Pace Willson, oral history interview with Bob Clark, March 7, 1994, SSAC.

25 "Program," Craft Guild of San Antonio, Third Regional Exhibition, November 4-25, 1962, Vertical Files, Witte Museum.

26 Margaret Pace Willson recalls that first meeting was held in November 1963 ("First Organization Meeting," manuscript notebook, SSAC), while typewritten notes in the Southwest School of Art and Craft archives indicate there were at least two meetings prior to that—one on May 16 and another sometime in August.

27 John Jockusch, interview with the author, July 26, 2000.

28 Margaret Pace Willson, oral history interview with Bob Clark, March 7, 1994, SSAC.

29 Margaret Pace Willson, statement at the time of Elizabeth (Betty) Urschel's death. SSAC.

30 The Art League held its first annual Art Jamboree, a fundraising project for local artists and craftsmen, in 1962. The event was held at the home of Tom Slick, half-brother of Charles Urschel, Betty Urschel's husband.

31 Helen Marie Hendrie, oral history interview with Bob Clark, May 11, 1994, SSAC.

32 La Sirena was located in a renovated building at 107 West Commerce Street that was owned by Marshall Steves. Early meetings were also held in the homes of needlepoint artist Janet Shook and Gloria Galt, who with her sister Patsy Steves, was an early supporter of the Craft Center.

33 Nancy Brown Negley [Wellin], oral history interview with Bob Clark, July 3, 1996, SSAC.

34 Hendrie, interview with Clark.

35 Articles of Incorporation, June 17, 1965, SSAC.

36 Mary Vance Green was a ceramic artist who had supervised the National Youth Administration craft program at La Villita. Green also served as secretary of the Southwest Craft Center in 1968-69. Joan Hixon was also a ceramic artist.

37 Nancy Brown Negley was the daughter of George R. Brown, joint owner of Brown and Root, a Houston-based construction and engineering company that, in the 1960s, was among the largest in the world. The Brown family established the Brown Foundation, Inc. Foundation records indicate that the grant, approved on October 5, 1965, was a general, unspecified contribution. Judy Crowhurst, Grant Assistant, the Brown Foundation, telephone interview with the author, July 28, 2000.

38 Edith McAllister, oral history interview with Bob Clark, October 13, 1994, SSAC.

39 Maggie Saunders Block, oral history interview with Bob Clark, February 18, 2000, SSAC; *San Antonio News,* September 4, 1967. The Brown Foundation grant was used to purchase a group of New England grave stone rubbings and a Latin American altarpiece. In 1967 the Southwest Craft Center loaned its three portfolios of original rubbings to the Witte Museum for exhibition, and their final disposition is unclear. The altarpiece was eventually sold to Ramona Seeligson, and the funds were used to renovate the center's facilities in La Villita.

40 McAllister, interview with Clark.

41 Fisher, *Saving,* 297.

42 Hendrie and Block, interviews with Clark.

43 Block served as president of the Southwest Craft Center in 1968, 1971-73, and 1977-78.

44 Block, interview with the author, April 6, 2001, SSAC.

45 Constructed according to plans by architect Robert H.H. Hugman, the project was officially turned over to the City of San Antonio on March 13, 1941. Fisher, *Crown Jewel,* 70.

46 The area was managed for the City of San Antonio's Parks Department by

Hamilton Magruder, who lived in the stone house at 420 Villita Street with his wife, school teacher Lydia Magruder. "Ham" Magruder, a much-loved and noted character, strived to maintain Maverick's vision. Magruder retired in 1964 and moved out of La Villita.

47 The study was conducted by Marco Engineering, a Los Angeles firm known for its design of Disneyland.

48 "Paseo del Rio San Antonio," promotional brochure. Nine years later Cyrus Wagner led the design team to propose development surrounding the Ursuline Academy buildings. Wagner's plan included restoration of the historic Ursuline buildings, a new office structure, and a parking garage. The $14.3 million project developed by the Southwest Craft Center, San Antonio Conservation Society, and San Antonio River Authority, was submitted for funding to the Department of Housing and Urban Development in 1972 but was rejected.

49 Margaret Pace Willson, interview with Clark.

50 Ibid. Willson tried to convince her mother to purchase a building on South Alamo Street that backed up to the San Antonio River. The structure was soon scheduled for demolition to make way for the Palacio del Rio Hotel, constructed for HemisFair '68.

51 Hendrie and Block to Frazer, January 3, 1968, SSAC. This letter indicates that Edith McAllister and Margaret Willson first discussed leasing the Magruder House with Robert Frazer, the City of San Antonio's director of Parks and Recreation, in November 1967.

52 McAllister, interview with Clark.

53 Block and Hendrie to Friend of the Arts, undated, SSAC.

54 SWCC Board Minutes, March 4, 1968, SSAC. Artists would receive 70% of the retail price of their objects, while the Craft Center received 30%.

55 Hendrie, interview with Clark.

56 Block to Robert Harris, March 13, 1968, SSAC. Robert "Bob" Harris was the son of Ethel Wilson Harris, resident manager of San José Mission from 1943 to 1968 and widely known for the crafts produced by her San José Pottery. Ethel Harris was a founder of the San Antonio Conservation Society and served as its president from 1951-53.

57 Volunteer Stevie Tucker went so far as to collect stones from the Guadalupe River to decorate the old kitchen sink as a display area.

58 With the exception of the Chrysanthemum Ball, staged annually by the Charity Ball Association, fundraising galas were not common in San Antonio in 1968.

59 SWCC Executive Committee Minutes, November 5, 1969, SSAC.

60 The house was located north of downtown on 417 Eighth Street between North Alamo Street and Avenue E in San Antonio's old Irish Flats neighborhood.

61 "Every Saturday Morning A Small Miracle Happens!" San Antonio Conservation Society Newsletter, January 1971.

62 SWCC Executive Board Minutes, July 24, 1969, SSAC.

63 SWCC Board Minutes, October 21, 1969, SSAC.

64 Fisher, Saving, 205. Ceramist Harding Black also worked with the NYA to

restore La Villita.

65 "They're discovering at the Southwest Craft Center," *San Antonio Light*, July 5, 1970.

66 President's Report," Southwest Craft Center, 1969, SSAC.

67 Undated press release, Southwest Craft Center [1970], SSAC; SWCC Board Minutes, January 19, 1970, SSAC. The board also approved paying gallery manager Jean Schoenig $450 per month beginning January 1, 1970, to assist in establishing and directing the newly established school. SWCC Board Minutes, November 12, 1969, SSAC.

68 Block to Clark, August 23, 1994, SSAC.

69 Invitation, March 20, 1970, SSAC.

The ART and CRAFT of PRESERVATION

1970-1975

At Home on the River

BY 1970, when the Southwest Craft Center marked the fifth anniversary of its founding, its core programs were defined and its course was set. The achievements were as notable as the speed with which they had been accomplished. The group had incorporated, solicited the participation of members and craftsmen, held fundraisers, opened a gallery, hired its first employees, and organized, presented, and sustained on-going educational programs for children and adults. Much of this work had been completed since late 1967, when the founders made their decision to open a gallery in conjunction with the six-month run of HemisFair '68.

The success of the Southwest Craft Center's gallery and educational programs created both challenges and new opportunities. In January 1970 Helen Marie Hendrie and Maggie Block visited a house in La Villita on Presa Street as the possible site for the center's adult craft classes. However, by the time the board met on June 8, 1970, other options were under consideration. Margaret Willson led a discussion

The Ursuline Academy's 19th century structures required extensive restoration by the middle 1960s. The dormitory (*above*) and the first academy (*facing page*) were miraculously saved from the fire that destroyed the 1910 academy building. The Southwest Craft Center acquired the dormitory in 1971 and the first academy in 1974.
Southwest School of Art and Craft.

about the need and demand of artists for nominally priced workshop space. "It was emphasized that creativity begets creativity with integrated proximity to fellow artists and craftsmen." A building in Olmos Park on the city's near north side that could provide suitable space was considered. Patsy Steves raised another possibility. The San Antonio Conservation Society had purchased a part of the old Ursuline Academy downtown on the San Antonio River. Steves wondered if the society would be amenable to leasing the space for a nominal fee to promote the goals of the Southwest Craft Center. She promised to confer with Conservation Society representatives and report her findings.[1]

The idea of using the old Ursuline Academy for the Southwest Craft Center had actually first been suggested on September 22, 1965, shortly after the center incorporated and the San Antonio Conservation Society purchased part of the property. An unsigned letter drafted to Conservation Society President Peggy Tobin stated, "It is our belief that a portion of the property formerly owned by the Ursuline

Order could be utilized for the active arts and eventually encompass all of the arts. We would like for you to consider apportioning a part of this space for the Southwest Craft Center . . . It would be our pleasure to meet with you at your earliest convenience."[2] If such a discussion actually took place in 1965, there is no record, and five years elapsed before the proposal was seriously pursued.

It was July 1970 before the board of the Southwest Craft Center formally adopted a motion to study the feasibility of establishing the Saturday Morning Discovery Program at the old Ursuline Academy.[3] Later that summer the San Antonio Conservation Society board directed its president, Vivian Hamlin, to discuss possible use of the buildings with Craft Center representatives. On September 10, 1970, at a meeting held in Betty Urschel's home, Hamlin outlined a proposal for the center's occupancy of the property. She and Helen Marie Hendrie, the center's president at the time, recalled that the offer was greeted with hesitancy as members expressed concerns about the condition and safety of the

Southwest Craft Center board members Carolyn Brown Negley, Maggie Saunders Block, Helen Marie Hendrie, and Mary Vance Green visited the dilapidated buildings following their acquisition. *Southwest School of Art and Craft.*

property.[4] After some discussion Margaret Willson, who had long envisioned a craft center on the San Antonio River, moved that the board accept the Conservation Society's invitation to relocate its school to the Ursuline Academy. Seconding Willson's motion was Bob Winn, who had hosted the center's organizers many times in its formative years.[5] The proposed agreement called for the Craft Center to simply furnish, occupy, and maintain the buildings in lieu of rent for two years. When the motion passed, a new era began.

A Loom and Two Students

Although the Southwest Craft Center's lease was not finalized for several months, classes began at the Ursuline Academy only six weeks after the move was approved. Because of the condition of the buildings, the Craft Center's first instructors and their students were, of necessity, somewhat intrepid. Kay Maxham, the first artist to move from La Villita, wrote

on October 26, 1970, "The first weaving class at old Ursuline started this morning with two students." She remarked that the students had difficulty finding their way to the patio, and though the studio had a lock, upon leaving for the day, she would "remove all scissors, tools, and sharp objects."[6] Maxham was soon joined by others who had taught at La Villita, including painter Diane Hendrie Harlow and stitchery artist Mary Heickman. Ceramist Bob Farmer, called by Maggie Block, " a brave potter" and a "hero," also began to teach at the Ursuline site. Farmer wore many hats, including de facto security guard, while single handedly establishing the center's ceramics department. He acquired equipment, planned and taught classes, and built the first gas-fired kiln, all in exchange for lodging, studio space, and a small salary.[7]

Slowed only slightly by the holidays, Helen Marie Hendrie mailed a letter the day after Christmas summoning the board to a January 5 meeting at the Ursuline Academy to "make plans for the future development of the Southwest Craft Center Creative Arts School."[8] The fact that it was a cold January did not deter the members, but as they met some might have wondered why they had chosen this site. Overcoming any reservations, members voted unanimously to adopt Maggie Block's motion to lease the old Ursuline convent on Augusta Street for two years.

Temperatures the following week fluctuated between 14 and 55 degrees, but when Saturday Morning Discovery convened at the new site for the first time on January 9, the warm reception undoubtedly overcame the chilly classroom. Maggie Block recalled how cold it was that first winter when they enlisted Helen Marie Hendrie's friend Madelyn Wilson as a part-time secretary. "I can just see her sitting there. There was one little string with one little light bulb, down where the weavers are, and here was Madelyn sitting at the desk—she was a tiny person—with her coat and her gloves on, typing! Because we didn't have any heat."[9] The weather was the first of many challenges Craft Center members would face at their new home, and it did not stop them.

Realizing the Vision

When asked about the problems encountered during the early days of the Southwest Craft Center, members invariably recall their financial struggles. Maggie Block remembered, "It was a lot of hard work to

Top: Weaver Kay Maxham began teaching at the Southwest Craft Center in 1968 and held the school's first class at the Ursuline site on October 26, 1970. *Southwest School of Art and Craft.*

Above: Bob Farmer came to teach at the Southwest Craft Center in 1969 and became not only the potter in residence, but also the Center's construction supervisor, security guard, and janitor. *Southwest School of Art and Craft.*

figure out how we were going to just be solvent."[10] The move to the Ursuline Academy required the volunteers not only to operate the growing school but also to find the funds to pay utilities and insurance and furnish and repair the old buildings. Though the Conservation Society remained committed to maintaining the site and rehabilitating the buildings, it too was limited by budget. Maggie Block regularly sent her yardman to mow the Craft Center's grounds and turned off lights to conserve the organization's scarce resources. She was known to remark, "No matter how lofty the hope, we realize how important the bottom line is!" [11]

Block and the other Craft Center volunteers relied constantly on their energy and creativity to overcome what appeared, on occasion, to be insurmountable challenges, and in the process created a whirlwind of activity. Artists, some of whom lived at the school, taught their classes in both the historic buildings and the gardens, and dramatic and dance groups performed in Ursuline chapel. Remembering the resounding echoes of Ballet Folklorico dancers, Maggie Block marveled that it was "a miracle that the stones held together! Dozens of tiny girls in black leotards scampered about the grounds. It was a delightful sight!"[12]

In late 1970, when the Southwest Craft Center became a tenant in the San Antonio Conservation Society's old Ursuline Academy buildings, developer Link Cowen still owned the majority of the 4.3-acre site. Cowen wanted a high price for his land and buildings, but when he died in 1971 his heirs were eager to sell and the cost dropped significantly. At that point the Conservation Society leapt into action to secure as much of the site as it could afford.

The Conservation Society was successful in purchasing another 23,000 square feet of the property, including the rest of the first academy building, the first academy addition, and the small building that had served as the academy's first chapel (today called the Emily Edwards Gallery). The remaining land and buildings were sold by the Cowen estate to parking lot operator W.J. Appedole. Appedole used the vacant area for a parking lot and leased the old laundry building (today a portion of Club Giraud) to the Southwest Craft Center for its ceramics studio. The portion of the dormitory building owned by Appedole remained boarded up.[13]

Above: In the Southwest Craft Center's early years, volunteers wore many hats, ranging from fund raiser to gardener. Founder Maggie Block took time out from board duties to weed the inner courtyard. *Southwest School of Art and Craft, courtesy of Maggie Block.*

Top Left: San Antonio's Ballet Folklorico, invited by the San Antonio Conservation Society to practice and perform in the Ursuline Academy's chapel, provided a use for the site and attracted visitors during the late 1960s and early 1970s. *Southwest School of Art and Craft.*

Bottom Left: The Ursuline Academy was a central feature of several redevelopment plans proposed in the early 1970s. In this 1971 drawing, urban designer Cyrus Wagner envisioned the restored Ursuline across the river from new luxury apartments that were finally built in 1979. *San Antonio* Express-News.

Asphalt parking lots and overgrown gardens lay beyond the 19th century buildings and walls when the Southwest Craft Center moved to the Ursuline Academy. *North San Antonio Times.*

Southwest Craft Center board members were anxious to purchase Appedole's section of the dormitory, and Maggie Block approached the president of the nearby National Bank of Commerce to discuss a proposal. Looking down at the Ursuline site from his offices, the banker, whom the Craft Center counted among its friends and supporters, was aghast. Block proudly toured him through the dormitory, which even she admitted was "boarded up and falling to pieces." His response was "'Oh, Maggie, if anybody tries to give it to you, say no.' He was just horrified!"[14]

"No" was not in Maggie Block's vocabulary, and undaunted she and other volunteers began to raise money. Through a generous donation from Mayor Walter McAllister and his wife Clio, the board of the Southwest Craft Center signed a six-month option on June 10, 1971, for $6,800, 10% of the dormitory's purchase price.[15] The McAllister's donation was followed by the largest gift in the organization's short history. Charles Urschel understood well the commitment of his wife and her friends to the Southwest Craft Center's goals. Through his gen-

The Ursuline dormitory was acquired by the Southwest Craft Center from W.J. Appedole in 1971, through the generosity of Betty and Charles Urschel. The Urschels joined Helen Marie Hendrie, Maggie Block, and Appedole (left to right) at the ceremonial transfer. *San Antonio* News.

erosity, purchase of the dormitory became a reality. This major step, culminating an exhausting and exciting year, was announced in the local press on Christmas Eve 1971.[16]

W.J. Appedole was an investor in parking lots, not old buildings, and he sought to divest himself of the remaining 2.5 acres of his Ursuline property. Though the Southwest Craft Center had just pur-

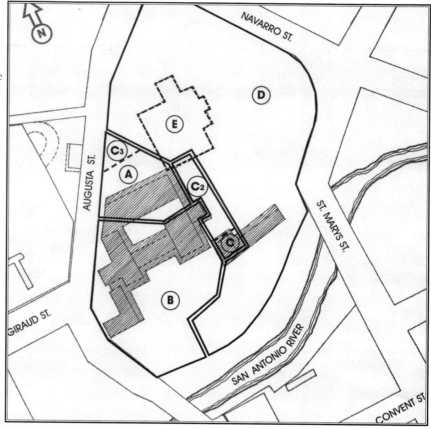

The entire 4.3 acre Ursuline Academy site was assembled by the Southwest Craft Center as follows: Parcel A (1971); Parcel B (1975); Parcels C and C2 (1973); Parcels C3 and D (1981). "E" denotes the location of the 1910 academy building destroyed by fire in 1967.

chased the dormitory and assumed a tremendous financial responsibility, members and their advisors were committed to buying additional buildings and land to assure access and parking for the school. In January 1972 they discussed a proposal to offer Appedole $102,000 for a portion of his property. Walter Mathis, a local stockbroker who was advising the organization, was enthusiastic, stating emphatically, "We'll raise the money!" Banker John Bennett was less optimistic and thought the chances of success were slim.[17] True to its commitment the Craft Center board authorized Mathis and Bennett to offer Appedole $10,000 for a one-year option.

Ultimately, in 1974, W.J. Appedole sold his remaining tract not to the Southwest Craft Center, but to Carolyn Brown Negley, who purchased it as an investment for $1 million.[18] Carolyn Negley had friends in both the San Antonio Conservation Society and the Southwest Craft Center. Although the property now had three owners, for the first time since the two organizations gained title, their third partner was a friend and fellow San Antonian.

An Exciting Happening

While Southwest Craft Center board members were still considering their options for expansion in La Villita, they enlisted a volunteer for life. In 1969 Maggie Block and Helen Marie Hendrie invited their friend Ruth Johnson to explore the old house on South Presa Street that they were considering for additional classroom space. When fate intervened and the Conservation Society offered the Craft Center use of the old Ursuline Academy, Ruth Johnson found a lifelong career. She was given the unglamorous task of filling the buildings with donated furniture and equipment, and she rose to the assignment with a fervor that was unabated for 27 years.

While Maggie Block developed organizational plans, Ruth Johnson joined her as a fundraiser extraordinaire, identifying sympathetic donors willing to support restoration of the center's new campus. Block remembered Ruth and Stewart Johnson transporting 16 friends at a time to the Ursuline in their "mountain wagon" for picnic suppers to acquaint them with the new project. "Romantic setting notwithstanding, some of the men thought we were insane!" Of their relationship, Block said, "Ruth and I spent those 27 years together. Her field was the 'historic restoration' and the acquisition of funds needed for projects. I assisted her whenever and wherever I could, sometimes 'smoothing feathers' and running interference."[19]

Following acquisition of the dormitory in December 1971, the center's board appointed Ruth Johnson chairman of the Craft Center's Historic Preservation Committee and charged her with renovating the historic building. Maggie Block laughed, "A great title, but we had no money!" It was therefore often a thankless task. Block, always alert for ways to stretch the organization's meager resources, had secured the services of minimum-wage summer workers through two public programs, CETA and SANYO.[20] She recalled with amusement Ruth Johnson's expression upon arriving to supervise her crew. "Ruth took one look at the gang, and said: 'I'll see you in the fall!'" Johnson was only briefly daunted, however, and returned to complete the dormitory renovation.

Others were enlisted in the cause as well, among them Evelyn Berg, who was elected to the board at its first meeting at the Ursuline

Maggie Block, Edith McAllister, and City Councilman Cliff Morton (left to right) cut the ribbon at the dedication of the completed dormitory building in October 1973, following almost two years of restoration. *San Antonio* Light.

Restoration of the Ursuline Academy was accomplished through the generosity of many individuals, the San Antonio Conservation Society, the Southwest Craft Center, the Department of Housing and Urban Development, the Texas Historical Commission, and the City of San Antonio. *Southwest School of Art and Craft.*

Academy in January 1971 and later served as president. Berg had moved to San Antonio in 1968 and, like other Southwest Craft Center volunteers, had a wealth of organizational experience and a deep affection for the arts. Though her first love was music, Berg was quickly recruited to the Craft Center's cause and given a challenging assignment soon after the move to the old Ursuline. Although the buildings were barely habitable, the group optimistically charged Berg with drafting policies and fees for use of the property by community groups. In doing so she laid the groundwork for the site-rental program that would become an invaluable source of revenue for the Southwest Craft Center.[21]

Under Ruth Johnson's watchful eye, and through the generosity of the Texas Historical Commission, City of San Antonio, and the Craft Center's friends and supporters, the first phase of the dormitory project was completed in less than two years, and the subsequent basement renovation was finished in 1975. Donors to the dormitory project included individuals who would give time and again to accomplish the goals of the Southwest Craft Center. They included Kathleen Alexander, Evelyn and Tom Berg, Carolyn Brown Negley, Frederick C. Hixon, and Elizabeth (Betty) Huth Coates. Coates' gift to assure renovation of the dormitory's first floor for arts and crafts education was the first of two major projects that honored her mother, Theresa O'Farrell Huth, and aunt, Clare O'Farrell Cantu, both Academy alumnae.[22]

When the dormitory restoration was well underway, Maggie Block wrote to a friend in February 1973, expressing the Southwest Craft Center's gratitude to the San Antonio Conservation Society for its efforts to save the old Ursuline. "The Conservation Society deserves much credit and gratitude for the imagination and generosity to turn the buildings over to an 'art organization.' They are responsible for making possible an exciting happening!" The ribbon was cut and the public was welcomed to the renovated dormitory on October 3, 1973.[23]

A Work in Progress

As operators of a growing school, Southwest Craft Center board members were energized rather than exhausted. They simultaneously raised funds, supervised construction, and planned and publicized

Ruth Johnson, chairman of the Southwest Craft Center's Historic Restoration Committee, was assisted by others including Walter Mathis, Betty Coates, and Maggie Block (left to right). *Southwest School of Art and Craft.*

"A Thing of Beauty Is a Joy Forever"

Ruth Johnson devoted 27 years of her life to the Southwest Craft Center, her work cut short by her untimely death in 1997. In the course of over a quarter century, Johnson's contributions included renovation of the nineteenth century convent buildings and development of the adjacent gardens. She once wrote to her fellow board members, "I'm not at all sure I'm glad that you got me to love SWCC so much!!" It was a love affair that began in January 1970 as the center's board considered expanding its facilities in La Villita. Helen Marie Hendrie and Maggie Block invited Johnson to become involved in restoring a dilapidated house owned by the City of San Antonio. The project was soon replaced by a grander dream to occupy and preserve the abandoned Ursuline Academy. When the Southwest Craft Center moved to the Ursuline site in January 1971, Johnson accepted the unglamorous job of collecting donated items to furnish the buildings. She never looked back. Johnson was architect, landscape architect, interior designer, and construction supervisor all rolled into one person. Her aesthetic vision guided renovation of the dormitory and chapel, construction of the Copper Kitchen, and creation of the center's gardens. No detail escaped her discerning eye as she chose mortar and paint colors, collected bricks and fencing, designed chandeliers and gazebos, and selected shrubs and trees. One contractor marveled, "I wish I could find and hire someone like Ruth." Johnson was persuasive and compelling as she shared her vision with potential donors, and their generosity turned dreams into realities. Above all, it was her friend Amy Shelton McNutt who shared Johnson's devotion to the center's buildings, grounds, and future. They planned and planted together, and McNutt, in recognition of Johnson's uncommon commitment, dedicated her final gift to her. Writing with care and deep personal knowledge, Amy McNutt inscribed her dedication plaque to read, Thanks to Ruthie Johnson, "*A thing of beauty is a joy forever.*"

classes and activities. Each member had her area of specialization—Maggie Block was the organizer and grant writer, Helen Marie Hendrie was adept at recruiting volunteers, and Ruth Johnson was the renovation expert. However, as the vision for the organization expanded these responsibilities increased proportionately, and the board hired Martha Fenstermaker as the school's full-time program director in October 1971.

Martha Fenstermaker was already involved in the Craft Center's work as one of the educators who had helped develop the Saturday Morning Discovery program.[24] She now assisted members of the board as they organized classes, hired craftsmen, wrote and administered the budget, prepared grant requests, and publicized the school's programs. Their hard work paid off, and by the summer of 1972, eighteen months after moving to the Ursuline, 226 students were enrolled in ceramics, film, metal, music, textiles, wood, and woodcarving. Classes were also offered in yoga, painting, and stained glass.[25]

The center's core curriculum was a work in progress, guided by student preferences, available equipment, and, sometimes, simple serendipity. When welding equipment was donated, the feasibility of a welding class was explored, and when woodworking proved popular Charles Urschel donated his woodworking equipment. Betty Urschel, seeing the need for more looms, ordered them made in California and shipped to San Antonio, and when Carolyn Brown Negley gave the center the old Ursuline cookhouse for its kiln room in March 1973 additional wheels were donated and purchased to accommodate more advanced classes.[26]

Beginning with the first adult classes held at La Villita and continuing at the Ursuline site, it was clear that ceramics, weaving, and photography would be keystones of the center's programming. The National Endowment for the Arts and major Texas foundations recognized the Southwest Craft Center in its first year at the Ursuline campus by funding artists' residencies in pottery and photography.[27] The popularity of courses offered under the direction of potter Bob Farmer and photographer Tom Wright helped sustain the Craft Center as it began to shape its long-range curriculum. When Farmer left in May 1972 to work in Colorado with acclaimed ceramic artist Paul Soldner, Steve Humphrey became the school's resident potter.

Top: Photographer Tom Wright had documented performances of the most popular rock bands of the day before settling in San Antonio as photographer in residence at the Southwest Craft Center. *Southwest School of Art and Craft.*

Bottom: Steve Humphrey became the school's potter in residence when Bob Farmer left the school in 1972 to work with Paul Soldner in Colorado. *Southwest School of Art and Craft, courtesy of Maggie Block.*

During this time it was not uncommon for artists to participate in both their artistic pursuits and construction work. Tom Wright had served as official photographer to some of the most renowned rock and roll stars of the day, but arriving at the Craft Center in 1972 he became both an instructor and the construction manager. Wright supervised unskilled workers employed under a government-funded training program as they removed plaster, stripped paint, and finished floors.28 Steve Humphrey, like his predecessor Bob Farmer, constructed kilns, helped maintain the facilities, and taught classes. Humphrey and Wright still found time in their busy schedules to plan, teach, and mount exhibits of their work.

Kathy Vargas, who later became nationally known for her photographs,, first registered for classes at the Craft Center after seeing pictures printed by a colleague studying with Tom Wright. At the time the center was "the roughest of facilities," a place where students and instructors constantly trailed in and out of studios against the backdrop of loud music. Vargas remembered that Wright, who taught advanced classes, never hesitated to instruct beginning students in basic techniques. His teaching methods engaged people, and they returned again and again. She described an atmosphere of creative exchange between artists and students of different media that was "totally active and interactive." At the Craft Center students of all disciplines gathered in the studios and gardens to share ideas, and students were inspired by the working professionals who were their teachers. "It was always in the back of our minds that we were studying in order to work our way to the level of professionalism." It was, she recalled, "a totally enlivening, encouraging experience."29

Lovingly Given

The old Ursuline Academy buildings owned by Carolyn Negley included the modest, deteriorated structures east of the first academy that overlooked the San Antonio River (today the Club Giraud). Sister Mary Augustine Joseph had written in October 1852 that this portion of the convent grounds contained "a kitchen, storeroom, fowl house and back apartments occupied by the gardener, his wife (our laundress)

and child."[30] In the course of over a hundred years, the structures had been variously used as a kitchen, laundry, workshop, music room, carriage house, and garage. Now under new ownership, the riverside buildings awaited their next use.

While Carolyn Negley was interested in developing her property, she was also well acquainted with the Southwest Craft Center's work. She could not help but be aware of the burgeoning ceramics program because the center's kiln stood adjacent to her land near the dormitory. On March 22, 1973, it was learned that Carolyn Negley would donate the building closest to the first academy—the old cookhouse—to the Craft Center to house a new pottery kiln and "other appropriate activities." She made only one stipulation—that the building be dedicated in honor of her mother-in-law. "I would like a plaque on the front wall to read: In memory of Laura Burleson Negley, lovingly given by Carolyn Brown Negley."[31] Negley, who had also assisted with renovating the dormitory, made this second expression of her generosity, but it would not be her last.[32]

The Ursuline Academy's outlying buildings had served various functions including kitchen, storeroom, workshop, carriage house, music room, laundry, and chicken house. The structures were acquired by Carolyn Brown Negley in 1974, sold to the Southwest Craft Center in 1979, and restored to house Club Giraud. The club was formed in 1981 to provide ongoing financial support to the school. *Southwest School of Art and Craft.*

Raising Enrollment and Eyebrows

When Martha Fenstermaker left the Southwest Craft Center in August 1973 to return to teaching, the board selected Marcie Baer (Larsen) as the center's administrator and program director. An experienced educator, Larsen had directed arts and crafts programs at various United States Army facilities.[33]

Marcie Larsen arrived to find a dynamic scene. Student enrollment totaled 310 in 50 classes, the first phase of the dormitory renovation was complete, site work was ongoing, and the board was had already begun to consider purchasing the Conservation Society's property. Graphic arts and glass had been incorporated into the curriculum and the jewelry department was expanding. Creative, energetic, and unfazed by this whirlwind, Larsen introduced new classes and programs, among them glass blowing and life drawing with nude models, the latter raising some eyebrows, together with attendance.[34]

At the end of three full years of operation at the Ursuline site, the craft school was experiencing a deficit in spite of rising enrollment. Tuition could not possibly cover operating expenses that approached $12,000 a month by mid-1974. The school clearly needed more students as well as other sources of earned income to fund its operations and maintenance. This reality, and the possibility of purchasing the Conservation Society's property, was the focus of four executive committee meetings in October and November 1974. Analyzing its programming commitment and financial position, the Craft Center's executive committee reiterated the center's primary goal— "to provide a first quality school for the creative arts in an atmosphere that encouraged creativity as well as productivity." Members also considered the restored school buildings as "a gift to the people of the United States." Future fundraising would focus on these dual purposes—the support and expansion of programming and maintenance of the treasured Ursuline site. [35]

A Home to Call Its Own

The Southwest Craft Center and the San Antonio Conservation Society had negotiated a new 15-year lease in March 1973 when their original 2-year agreement expired. One issue remained unresolved—a

The Southwest Craft Center's old kiln yard was later replaced with a modern ceramics studio that was dedicated in 1982 and named for Edith McAllister. *Southwest School of Art and Craft.*

convoluted property line devised in 1965 to separate the chapel owned by the Conservation Society from the part of the dormitory that was then owned by Link Cowen. The line had been drawn to assure the integrity of the chapel's rear wall in the event that the adjoining dormitory was demolished. When the Southwest Craft Center acquired the remainder of the dormitory in late 1971, the irregular division became unnecessary.[36]

Buoyed by its success to date, the Southwest Craft Center's executive committee began to discuss acquisition of the San Antonio Conservation Society's property. Maggie Block had already broached the subject with Conservation Society president Beverly Blount, and on February 20, 1974, Craft Center president Edith McAllister was given approval to enter into negotiations. Only three years had elapsed since the Craft Center had moved to the site rent-free.[37]

At the time the Southwest Craft Center approached the Conservation Society, the society was waiting for news of its $136,000 grant application to the Economic Development Administration (EDA) for funding to restore the first academy building and to landscape the academy's grounds to the San Antonio River.[38] The society's request was approved in March 1974, marking the first time that an EDA grant had been awarded for historic preservation. The Craft Center and Conservation Society negotiated in the midst of ongoing construction.[39]

San Antonio Conservation Society president Beverly Blount, architect Brooks Martin, and Economic Development Agency representative Bob Farmer (left to right) broke ground on June 14, 1974, for the agency's $136,000 project to restore the first academy building and landscape the grounds to the river. *San Antonio Conservation Society.*

The Southwest Craft Center was unprepared to offset the Conservation Society's estimated $449,000 investment in the Ursuline site, but it was not asked to do so. The society initially proposed a selling price of $300,000, but after months of negotiations Edith McAllister announced at the September board meeting that the Conservation Society would sell the property to the center for $180,000. It was, McAllister stated, "a fair and generous price." [40]

Wary of high renovation and maintenance costs, Southwest Craft Center members nonetheless realized that ownership would allow them to set priorities and engage in financial planning rather than crisis budgeting. The future would be filled with challenges for board members, but they would be their own landlord with the ability to shape their own destiny. Enabled by the generosity of Adele Frost, who donated the entire purchase price, the Craft Center's board voted unanimously to submit a letter of intent to the Conservation Society.[41] When the contract was signed on New Year's Eve 1974, both organizations had achieved their goals. The Southwest Craft Center had a permanent home, and the San Antonio Conservation Society had assured the preservation, restoration, and adaptive use of the old Ursuline Academy.[42] Conservation Society president Beverly Blount wrote to Maggie Block, who had worked so hard to achieve this goal, "The buildings all seem so happy with all of the people in and out and all of the activities that are going on there now. I know that as your programs continue, it will become even a stronger focal point for the city of San Antonio."[43] The following summer when Craft Center president Evelyn Berg presented the Conservation Society a check completing the purchase, she was joined by former presidents Maggie Block and Edith McAllister. In an interesting turn of fate, Berg presented the check to another former Craft Center president, Nancy Negley, who had recently been elected president of the San Antonio Conservation Society.

"Strengthened by the Knowledge of Your Sheltering Wings"

The Southwest Craft Center now owned the majority of the old Ursuline's historic buildings, including its centerpiece, the 1867 Gothic Revival chapel. Eight months later Ruth Johnson announced that the chapel would be renovated with a gift from Betty Huth Coates. Her gift

Southwest Craft Center president Evelyn Berg presented a check to San Antonio Conservation Society president (and Craft Center founder) Nancy Brown Negley in July 1975 for purchase of the Society's Ursuline Academy holdings. *San Antonio Conservation Society.*

would again be made in honor of her mother and aunt, Theresa O'Farrell Huth and Clare O'Farrell Cantu.[44] Though not the oldest of the Ursuline buildings, the chapel was perhaps the most beloved of all the structures, and its renovation was carefully undertaken over several years.

When the board of the Southwest Craft Center purchased the San Antonio Conservation Society's holdings in 1974, it also established a group of supporters named the Ursuline Angels. The Angels group was the Craft Center's highest membership category, and its ranks included the organization's most dedicated donors and volunteers. Writing to members in August 1976 at the end of "a tumultuous first year of expansion in many directions," the Ursuline Angel Committee paused to express its gratitude. They had been, they said to their members, "strengthened by the knowledge of your sheltering wings."[45]

Restoration of the Ursuline Chapel was made possible through the generosity of Betty Coates (second from left) who studied plans with Ruth Johnson, Maggie Block, and architect Chris Carson (left to right). The chapel was named for Coates on the occasion of the school's 25th anniversary in 1991. *Southwest School of Art and Craft.*

The Ursuline Chapel

The Ursuline sisters worshipped for 17 years in a modest stone building adjoining their convent before undertaking construction of an impressive Gothic Revival chapel. The cornerstone of the new chapel was laid on January 20, 1867, and by April 1868 the San Antonio *Herald* reported that the "magnificent building" was nearly complete. For the first time the public could worship at the Ursuline convent, separated from the cloistered sisters by floor-to-ceiling lattice screens. The sisters, students, and local Catholics were called to services by the bell mounted high atop the adjacent dormitory. Recalling her days as a student at the turn of the twentieth century, Emily Edwards wrote fondly of the large statues, lighted candles, soft music, and incense that set the tone for daily Mass. The chapel remained the center of convent life until 1965 when the sisters sold the building and it was deconsecrated. Renovated through the generosity of Elizabeth (Betty) Huth Coates, the chapel was named in her honor when the Southwest School of Art and Craft celebrated its twenty-fifth anniversary in 1991. The chapel has continued to provide a central gathering place for both the school and the community at large.

The Angel Tapestry

Ruth Johnson and Betty Coates agreed that an appropriate focal point was needed to complete the Ursuline chapel renovation. In 1991 they commissioned San Antonio artist Zelime Matthews to design a needlepoint tapestry to adorn the soaring limestone walls. Rich in medieval traditions, the tapestry was decidedly Texan as well. Matthews chose the angel as the central design theme, noting that Emily Edwards wrote, "Angels seemed very present to us in the convent . . . Angels accused our wandering thoughts and deeds." Among symbols of the Ursuline Order and the convent buildings, an 8-foot angel overlooks the arching San Antonio River with 65 native wildflowers, 81 birds and butterflies, and 34 animals. In the medieval tradition the patron's initials are entwined in the sky, a fitting tribute to Betty Coates, who died in May 1996, shortly before the tapestry was dedicated.

The Angel Tapestry was designed by San Antonio artist Zelime Matthews to provide a focal point in the restored Ursuline chapel. *Southwest School of Art and Craft.*

Notes

1 SWCC Board Minutes, June 8, 1970, SSAC.

2 Undated, unsigned draft letter, ＿＿ to Mrs. Don Tobin, SSAC. No final copy of this letter has been located, and it is unclear if it was ever sent. Margaret Pace Willson's undated, handwritten journal titled "Southwest Craft Center, Early Planning Notes" (SSAC) includes the notation, "talk to Wanda about the Ursuline." Also included is a notation about a "Nov. 1966 craft show," indicating that the journal dates from the 1965-66 period.

3 SWCC Executive Committee Minutes, July 28, 1970, SSAC.

4 Hendrie and Hamlin, interview with the author, February 17, 2000, SSAC.

5 SWCC Board Minutes, September 10, 1970, SSAC.

6 Kay Maxham to Jean ＿＿＿, October 26, 1970, SSAC.

7 Block to the author, October 25, 2000, SSAC.

8 Hendrie to Southwest Craft Center Board Members, December 26, 1970, SSAC.

9 SWCC Board Minutes, January 5, 1971, SSAC. Joining board members at this important meeting were Dena Todd and Marianne Greenwood, representatives of the American Craft Council South Central Region.

10 Block, interview with Clark.

11 President's Report, November 2, 1978; SWCC Board Minutes, January 5, 1971, SSAC. The lease agreement between the Southwest Craft Center and the San Antonio Conservation Society required that Craft Center improvements must be approved by the society. The society was not bound to make improvements but was permitted to as its budget would allow.

12 Block to Clark, August 24, 1994, SSAC.

13 The San Antonio Conservation Society owned the western end of the dormitory that connected to the chapel.

14 Block, interview with Clark. The banker was Richard Calvert.

15 SWCC Board Minutes June 10, 1971, SSAC.

16 "Ursuline dormitory becomes Crafts Center," *San Antonio News*, December 24, 1971.

17 SWCC Board Minutes, January 19, 1972, SSAC. John Bennett was chairman of the board of the National Bank of Commerce (NBC) and was married to Eleanor Bennett, president of the San Antonio Conservation Society from 1953 to 1955. According to Maggie Block, it was ultimately John Bennett who was able to influence W.J. Appedole, operator of the NBC parking garage, to sell a portion of his property to the Southwest Craft Center.

18 Carolyn Brown Negley (Mrs. William Negley) and Nancy Brown Negley (Mrs. Alfred Negley) were married to cousins, and the Brown families were not related.

19 Block to SWCC Executive Board, February 27, 1995, SSAC.

20 CETA is the acronym for the Comprehensive Employment Training Act and

SANYO for the San Antonio Neighborhood Youth Organization.

21 SWCC Board Minutes, March 8, 1971, SSAC. Evelyn Berg's husband, Tom, was president of Friedrich Refrigerators, Inc., and donated window air conditioners to be used at La Casita where the Craft Center's first classes were held. Later the company was instrumental in cooling the Ursuline buildings.

22 SWCC Board Minutes, October 11, 1972, SSAC. Block to Nell _____, February 17, 1973, (SSAC) states that Coates promised Nancy Negley that she would restore the chapel. Though Coates, married at the time to Sam Maddux, was known as Betty Maddux, she is posthumously called Betty Coates, acknowledging her marriage to George Coates.

23 Block to Nell _____, February 17, 1973, SSAC; "Craft Center is dedicated at old Ursuline Convent," San Antonio *News*, October 4, 1973.

24 SWCC Board Minutes, October 20, 1971, SSAC; Martha Fenstermaker was also the niece of artist Mary Vance Green, who directed the NYA's crafts program in La Villita, and the great-niece of Rena Maverick Green, co-founder of the San Antonio Conservation Society.

25 SWCC Executive Committee Minutes, August 9, 1972, SSAC.

26 Before the kiln was completed, Bob Farmer left the Craft Center to study in Colorado with Paul Soldner and was succeeded by potter-in-residence Steve Humphrey.

27 The NEA Artists-in-Residence grants were matched by the Brown Foundation (ceramics) and the Ewing Halsell Foundation (photography).

28 Tom Wright had toured with The Who and counted other well known musicians among his friends.

29 Kathy Vargas, telephone interview with the author, July 4, 2001. Vargas is the chairman of the Art and Music Department at University of the Incarnate Word in San Antonio.

30 *Letters from the Ursuline*, 231. To the east the sisters had maintained a garden and established a cemetery and, in 1872, constructed a two-story stone building. These features and other small buildings along the river had been demolished for the extension of St. Mary's Street in 1914.

31 SWCC Board Minutes, March 22, 1973, SSAC. The building is sometimes referred to as the laundry and was called the "cook house" by Negley. It apparently served at various times both as a kitchen and a laundry. Laura Burleson Negley (Mrs. Richard Negley) was Carolyn Brown Negley's mother-in-law.

32 The property line separating the first academy building from the parking lot owned by Carolyn Negley was only six inches from the building. Negley subsequently donated a small strip of land to connect the kitchen/kiln with the academy building. SWCC Board Minutes, March 22, 1973, SSAC; Block, interview with Clark.

33 Interestingly, the army arts and crafts program was pioneered by General Frederick H. Osborn, brother of Aileen Osborn Webb, whose advice had helped guide the Craft Center's formation and development.

34 Marcie Larsen, interview with the author, July 29, 2000, SSAC.

35 SWCC Executive Committee Minutes, October-November 1974, SSAC. At the end of two years at the Ursuline campus, the Craft Center reported $30,000 in income and $46,000 in expenses. Though the loss was offset by other contributions, there was still a deficit of $2,000.

36 Block to Coates, January 30, 1973, SSAC; The Conservation Society's Ursuline Committee was chaired by Nancy Brown Negley, a founder and the first president of the Southwest Craft Center. When a lease extension and new dormitory property line were discussed, Negley was vocal in her objections to both propositions. She cited pending negotiations with the Department of Housing and Urban Development for restoration funds.

37 SWCC Board Minutes, February 20, 1974, SSAC; McAllister to Blount, February 25, 1974, SSAC.

38 SWCC Board Minutes, January 16, 1974, SSAC. The Conservation Society committed $34,000 to match the $136,000 grant request. This was the first time that E.D.A. funds had been granted for historic preservation purposes.

39 "U.S. funds will help restore Ursuline," San Antonio Light, March 3, 1974. Construction was underway in June 1974. SWCC Board Minutes, June 20, 1974, SSAC.

40 SWCC Board Minutes September 1974, SSAC; Fisher, Saving, 396. Whereas the Craft Center minutes state the society's estimate as $449,000, Fisher gives the amount as $500,000.

41 SWCC Board Minutes, September 1974, SSAC. Adele Frost had also made possible the Adele and Jack Frost Garden between the dormitory and cookhouse.

42 The final sale did not take place until June 30, 1975, upon completion of the EDA funded restoration. Federal and state grants to restore the Ursuline Academy required acceptance of deed restrictions to assure maintenance and preservation of the buildings.

43 Blount to Block, January 28, 1975, SSAC.

44 SWCC Board Minutes, February 19, 1976, SSAC; "A $250,000 project: Old Ursuline Academy chapel being restored," North San Antonio Times, December 2, 1976. As early as February 1973, when the Conservation Society still owned the chapel, Betty Coates had promised Nancy Negley that she would restore the building.

45 Ursuline Angel Committee to Ursuline Angels, August 1976, SSAC. Maggie Block recalls that the Ursuline Angels group was suggested by Bill Lende.

BEYOND BEGINNINGS

1976-2001

A Time of Unusual Growth

THE tenth anniversary of the Southwest Craft Center occurred in mid-1975, and there was scarcely time to take note of the occasion. During the organization's first ten years, members of the board had invested an extraordinary amount of time assuring that their school had a roof over its head, that there were funds to buy equipment, and that the staff and bills were paid. Purchase of the Conservation Society's property assured that fundraising for restoration, maintenance, and operations would consume the board's energy for the foreseeable future. Now, however, it was time to stop and re-visit the Craft Center's educational purpose.

In June 1975, several weeks before the purchase of the Conservation Society's property became final, Betty Urschel took the floor at a Southwest Craft Center board meeting. She reasoned that the buildings were well on their way to completion, and attention should now turn to programming, particularly the "departments of the school which are not yet as strong as weaving and ceramics."[1] Although restoration of the buildings remained an ongoing commitment, the members would have to continue to explore ways to improve programming.

Several months later Maggie Block wrote to William J. Brown,

Opposite left: Bob Fromme, who chaired the school's ceramics program in the 1970s, demonstrated for young people at a 1975 workshop. *Southwest School of Art and Craft.*

Opposite right: Ceramic sculptor Luis Guzman was a popular instructor for 18 years before returning to his native Chile in 1988. *Southwest School of Art and Craft.*

Opposite bottom left: Artists Wilanna and Bill Bristow taught at the school in its early years, and are seen here collaborating on a silkscreen design. *Southwest School of Art and Craft.*

Opposte bottom right: Watercolorist Caroline Shelton, known for her depictions of San Antonio's architecture and colorful celebrations, taught at the school for many years and generously donated works to be sold to support its programming. *Southwest School of Art and Craft.*

director of Penland School of Crafts. "We have a craft school attuned to Penland in spirit, though not yet arrived at the desired level of quality." She summarized the accomplishments of the past five years—35 part-time instructors teaching in ten departments with some 400 students in three sessions annually—and concluded by saying "the Craft Center is ready for the next important step forward."[2]

Some important steps were, in fact, taken. In 1976 a graduate of the Kansas City Art Institute named Dennis Smith arrived to assist potter Bob Fromme. It was unlikely that Smith realized he would remain for a quarter century to develop the school's nationally recognized ceramics program. Also in the late 1970s, Program Director Marcie Larsen had initiated a collaborative program with St. Philip's College, a branch of the city's community college system, that allowed students studying at the Craft Center to receive college credit. By September 1978 approximately 100 St. Philip's students attended classes in design, drawing, and ceramic design.[3] To further extend the institution's impact on the community, the center's gallery director, Caroline Tiemann, developed a commission program to assist artists in placing their work in private homes and businesses. Indicative of the school's growing stature, renowned artists, including Paul Soldner, Bob Ebendorf, Ted Hallman, Mary Walker Philips, Lois Brooks, Mary Heickman, Marvin Lipofsky, and Dale Chilhuly, had visited the Southwest Craft Center to demonstrate and teach their techniques.[4]

It was a time of "unusual growth," and to manage the Southwest Craft Center's development the board hired Dr. Merle Wachter as administrative director in March of 1977. Wachter had lived in Mexico since 1942 and, most recently, had served as dean of the University of the Americas Graduate School in Mexico City, overseeing an art department with 250 students.[5] Marcie Larsen remained as the center's program director for one more year and, when she left in April 1978, was applauded for "helping build the school with only a skeleton staff in the beginning."[6] In five years the Craft Center had grown from fewer than 1,000 students to 3,300 students, who participated in classes, workshops, and visiting artist seminars.

Supporting the Cause of Art

In spite of these advances in programming, the financial situation of the Southwest Craft Center was still precarious. Volunteers had engaged in a variety of traditional fundraising projects, including annual galas, sale of coupon books, auctions, waitressing in exchange for gratuities, and cruises that returned donations to the center. The Craft Center had also customarily opened its gallery and school to the public during San Antonio's annual Fiesta celebration in April.7 In 1973 a successful show and sale of students' work had provided income and exposure to both the artists and the school.

While these efforts kept the Southwest Craft Center's name before the public and produced some income, the board wanted to bring more visitors to the picturesque Ursuline site to acquaint them with the school and its purposes. Volunteers created an event they named the "Texas Folk Craft Experience," a two-day festival where artists produced and sold their works while visitors enjoyed food and music. Maggie Block reported that the first Texas Folk Craft Experience on August 10-11, 1974, brought "over 6,000 people to the Ursuline to admire our buildings, but also interested many, many people in the Craft Center classes."[8] The Folk Craft Experience was popular with visitors and did educate the public about the Southwest Craft Center and earn income for the organization. It was, however, held at the hottest time of the year and was often confused with the Institute of Texan Cultures' Texas Folklife Festival, another local celebration. Though the name and date of the event were changed, it still needed a more definitive identity to maximize its potential.

By the fifth year of the Folk Craft Experience in 1978, Southwest Craft Center volunteers were well experienced in the production of fairs.[9] Naomi Russell, who had served as chairman of the Conservation Society's annual fundraiser, A Night in Old San Antonio, understood well the components of a successful event. Russell felt that the Craft Center could build on its experience and redefine its fair. She proposed moving the event to coincide with the city's annual Fiesta celebration in April and changing its format to include juried and expanded craft exhibits, entertainment, and food. The new event, to be named the Fiesta Arts Fair, won official approval by the Fiesta Commission and opened its gates to the public for the first time on April 21, 1978.[10]

An Urban Oasis

The Craft Center's programs, special events, and ongoing restoration of its historic buildings gradually captured the public's attention and drew increasing numbers of visitors. In the first eight months of 1975 alone, over 42,000 people toured the site or attended functions there. To capitalize on those numbers, members reasoned that an attractive dining place with an appealing lunch menu would capture some visitors and serve downtown workers as well. Ruth Johnson set out to create just such a setting. With assistance from her friend and fellow gardener, Amy Shelton McNutt, Ruth Johnson planned, built, and equipped the restaurant and dining room that opened in September 1975 and was named the Copper Kitchen.[11]

The 1977 Folk Craft Experience included demonstrations of many art forms including a kite-making workshop by Pat Hammond. *Southwest School of Art and Craft, photo by Michael D. Johnson.*

Fiesta Arts Fair

Visitors have flocked to the Fiesta Arts Fair since the event first began under that name on the first weekend of Fiesta Week in 1978. Led by Craft Center board member Naomi Russell, volunteers took the best of their Texas Folk Craft Experience and created an event unlike any other on the crowded Fiesta calendar. As a veteran chairman of the San Antonio Conservation Society's A Night in Old San Antonio fundraiser, Russell knew well the elements of a successful event and worked with chairmen for nine years to fine-tune the Fiesta Arts Fair. The fair's signature elements—juried exhibits with artists selling a wide range of high-quality crafts, demonstrations, music, food, and drinks—have remained largely unchanged since the inception. Only the scope has changed. Once confined to the old Ursuline Academy's historic buildings and courtyards, the Fiesta Arts Fair has gradually spread to encompass the center's entire parking lot. Committee members who used to haul platforms, hammer nails, and cook a variety of dishes now coordinate over 500 community volunteers. The event, that up to 1983 produced less than $20,000 in income, has grown into the organization's largest fundraiser and attracts artists from throughout the nation. Looking back, early Fiesta Arts Fair volunteers marvel at the tasks they performed, but all agree that they did it out of devotion to the common goal they shared with their friends—to earn money to support the programs of the Southwest Craft Center.

Top: The Fiesta Arts Fair succeeded the Folk Craft Experience in 1978 and offered visitors the opportunity to purchase high-quality crafts by artists from throughout the United States. *Southwest School of Art and Craft.*

Bottom: The vision and enthusiasm of Ruth Johnson (left) and Amy Shelton McNutt (right) helped to restore the historic Ursuline buildings and landscape the school's gardens and courtyards in the years between 1975 and 1983. *Southwest School of Art and Craft.*

Top: Lupe Padilla began to serve her famous enchiladas to Southwest Craft Center volunteers in 1971 shortly after the school moved to the Ursuline Academy. She celebrated her 30th anniversary in 2001. *Southwest School of Art and Craft.*

Right: The Copper Kitchen, opened in 1974 to attract lunchtime diners to the Southwest Craft Center, took its name from the collection of copperware donated by Amy Shelton McNutt. *Southwest School of Art and Craft.*

This was only the first of several projects that Ruth Johnson and Amy Shelton McNutt, affectionately known as "Momma Mac," undertook together. Amy McNutt, an avid gardener, was also famous for the hospitality and food enjoyed by international visitors to her Gallagher Ranch north of San Antonio. Johnson and McNutt's collaborations between 1975 and 1983 transformed the center's buildings and grounds into a lush haven amid the bustle of downtown San Antonio.

Copper Kitchen

Southwest Craft Center volunteers, members, and supporters had dined in the buildings and on the grounds of the old Ursuline Academy since the center's move to the site in 1971. There were few restaurants nearby, and of necessity board members began to bring picnics and prepare meals to sustain themselves during the long renovation process. In fair weather they ate under the courtyard's spreading trees at makeshift picnic tables. Craft Center instructors and downtown workers strolling by often stopped to talk, view the progress, and occasionally join in a meal. When Maggie Block enlisted Lupe Padilla to feed the volunteers, a legend was born. Still, a proper kitchen was needed, and Ruth Johnson began to plan. In December 1974 she reported to the board that research and planning for a kitchen in the newly dedicated dormitory was completed. Johnson and her friend Amy Shelton McNutt, a dedicated and renowned cook, joined together to plan and furnish the kitchen. When it was completed in 1974, McNutt donated her personal collection of copperware to decorate the room, giving it the name the "Copper Kitchen." The Rock Room, across the hall, was furnished as a dining room with Texas pine tables and chairs, and the Copper Kitchen opened its doors to the public in September 1975. Lupe Padilla was there that first day to cook her famous enchiladas and other recipes for a steady stream of visitors, and a quarter century later she continues to serve appreciative lunch crowds.

Amy Shelton McNutt

Amy Shelton McNutt was well known for her hospitality, imaginative food, and gardens long before Ruth Johnson introduced her to the Southwest Craft Center. Together with her husband, V.H. McNutt, "Momma Mac" (as she was affectionately called), owned and operated the internationally known Gallagher Ranch north of San Antonio. There she entertained visitors from throughout the world, introducing them to the Hill Country landscape and South Texas cuisine. While her friend Ruth Johnson was supervising renovation of the old Ursuline dormitory in 1973, McNutt became intrigued with the project. Maggie Block described it as the meeting of a "creative cook" and a "builder." McNutt thought that the creative art center needed a gathering spot, and together McNutt and Johnson planned, designed, and equipped the Copper Kitchen and adjacent dining room. The completed project was celebrated in conjunction with McNutt's eighty-sixth birthday on August 24, 1975, beginning an annual tradition that marked Momma Mac's ongoing generosity to the Southwest Craft Center until her death in October 1983. As Ruth Johnson planned throughout the next eight years, McNutt's birthday gifts transformed the center's grounds with lighting, fencing, trees, and shrubs. She made possible bricking of porches, landscaping of the convent garden, creation of the river garden and its signature gazebo, and the Club Giraud garden and its gazebo. Always conscious of the center's public face, McNutt beautified asphalt parking lots as well as service areas and, to assure ready availability of plants, constructed a greenhouse. The Garden Room, a hospitality center where volunteers could greet visitors and share information about the old Ursuline Academy and Craft Center, was planned before McNutt's death and dedicated in her honor in 1987. Before her death Amy Shelton McNutt marked her ninety-fourth birthday with the greatest of her gifts to the Southwest Craft Center—a $1 million endowment to assure the perpetual maintenance of the Southwest Craft Center gardens. Acknowledging her friend, who gave unselfishly so that others could enjoy this special place, Ruth Johnson wrote, "she taught us much about beauty and love and about making dreams become realities."

Ruth Johnson, Amy Shelton McNutt, and other Southwest Craft Center members were gifted gardeners who understood that lushly landscaped grounds would attract visitors and provide a highly marketable setting for special events. Beautification of the site to enhance its wonderful architecture and attract visitors was a well-founded strategy. Though the Craft Center's buildings were charming, they adjoined a sea of asphalt and unkempt frontage along the San Antonio River. Adele Frost, who just the year before had made it possible for the Center to purchase the Conservation Society's holdings, assured that the school would be shielded from the unattractive parking lots to the north and east. Under garden chairman Margaret Deeley's guidance, a brick terrace and garden was created adjoining the dormitory building. Planted with trees and shrubs and decorated with antique ironwork donated by members, the garden was dedicated to the memory of Frost's late husband, Jack.[12]

The Conservation Society's EDA grant had funded landscaping of the convent garden and construction of a limestone patio adjacent to the first academy building. This had quickly become a popular site for community and social gatherings, but beyond the patio and old convent wall lay a dirt parking lot piled with rocks and construction debris overlooking the San Antonio River. In July 1978 Ruth Johnson announced that Amy Shelton McNutt would like to donate a new river

The Ursuline gardens have been a place for retreat and recreation since the convent was established on the banks of the San Antonio River in 1851. Where the sisters once meditated, students of all ages now come to join in the artistic process, and visitors stroll and gather for community celebrations. After 150 years, the tree-shaded grounds remain a quiet oasis from the bustle of the city. *Southwest School of Art and Craft*

garden to the Craft Center. Johnson envisioned what others could not see and created a terraced garden with a pavilion, attractive fences and walls, and mature landscaping. To complete the project, members who had long dreamed of a river entrance and boat landing took the opportunity to gain the city's commitment to provide barge access to the Craft Center.[13] The completed project was presented as a gift from McNutt to the Craft Center in August 1979. Once again, visitors would enjoy the beauty of this portion along the San Antonio River where the Ursuline sisters had strolled.

Although the Southwest Craft Center's galleries and Copper Kitchen showed modest profits in early 1979, monthly expenses of $20,000 continued to far exceed income.[14] Faced with a deficit the board nonetheless remained committed to owning the entire old Ursuline site. A committee chaired by Margaret Tobin was formed to approach Carolyn Brown Negley about purchasing her property, which included the buildings along the San Antonio River and the parking lot, and in July 1978 it was reported that Negley's asking price was $943,000.[15] It was a generous offer without profit to Negley, who had held the land since 1974. Members determined that they would raise $643,000 and borrow $300,000 to purchase the land by January 23, 1979, and their plan succeeded.[16] Only eight years after the Southwest Craft Center had made its first small purchase of Ursuline property, it was now the owner rather than tenant of the entire 4.3-acre site that the sisters had sold 14 years before.

Carrying the Banner

Merle Wachter remained at the Craft Center during this critical period, and then announced in February 1979 that he would return to teaching.[17] To replace Wachter the board searched for a person who had organizational and financial experience, an artistic background, and connections to a network of peers. In May, four months after Wachter's departure, the board hired Darrell Bohlsen, founding director of the Sangre de Cristo Arts and Conference Center in Pueblo, Colorado, as the center's new director.[18] Block, who was serving her third term as Craft Center president, wrote, "Probably none can be and do everything. But we think Darrell will try!"[19]

Right: San Antonio potter and ceramics instructor Bertie Smith worked with the school from its earliest days in La Villita. She was among the first teachers at the Ursuline campus in 1971 and remains active 30 years later. *Southwest School of Art and Craft.*

Bottom left: A young student learns to paint in the Saturday Morning Discovery program. *Southwest School of Art and Craft.*

Bottom right: Graphics instructor Lee Newbury organized the school's first printmaking workshop in 1976. *Southwest School of Art and Craft.*

Southwest Craft Center board members Helen Marie Hendrie, Maggie Block, and Edith McAllister *(left to right)* gleefully tear up the school's mortgage after making the final payment in March 1981. *San Antonio* Light.

Bohlsen arrived during a time of tight budgeting and careful planning. Eighteen months after coming to the Southwest Craft Center, he summarized the center's short- and long-range goals. Salary issues and improvements to studios were of immediate concern, while in the long term he recommended that the center "carry the banner for crafts by whatever ways our resources permit."[20] To this end Bohlsen focused programming by narrowing the curriculum and organizing classes into five departments—metals, clay, fibers, photography, and fine arts.

In the late 1970s and early 1980s, the board of the Southwest Craft Center explored ways to broaden and increase its audience and assure long-term financial viability. After analyzing various options, including the exhibition of two museum quality collections, it was decided that the school's limited space and small staff would be devoted to its core purpose and mission. [21]

Accordingly, two important decisions were made. First, to free itself of encumbrances, the board raised the funds to pay off its note on the property and, by February 1981, owned the Ursuline property free and clear. [22] The board also entertained a new idea. "Baker Duncan and Bill Lende proposed using the river buildings as a private club, with dues and a tax deductible contribution to the Southwest Craft Center."[23] This idea was modeled after the exclusive Argyle Club that had been

Edith McAllister dons a hard hat decorated with a model of the historic clock tower at the groundbreaking for the school's new ceramics studio that was later named in her honor. *Southwest School of Art and Craft, courtesy of Maggie Block.*

organized in 1955 to benefit the Southwest Foundation for Research and Education.[24] This positive and creative solution to supporting the work of the Southwest Craft Center was embraced, and by September 1981 an endowment fund was established to receive donations from the new club that was named in honor of the school's original architect, François Giraud.[25]

It was Edith McAllister who took charge of the Club Giraud project, raising funds and overseeing the project to renovate the crumbling riverside buildings. Construction of Club Giraud also necessitated moving the kilns located in the building donated by Carolyn Brown Negley. As owners of the entire site, the Craft Center could now choose a preferred location for them, and the new ceramics studio was constructed north of the Frost Garden.

After 11 years the Southwest Craft Center finally had a dedicated clay facility with studios, five gas-fired kilns, and drying, glazing, and storage rooms. At its dedication on June 1, 1982, Ceramics Department chairman, Dennis Smith, presented retiring president Edith McAllister with a commemorative plate designed by veteran Craft Center artist Luis Guzmán.[26] The assembled crowd, in gratitude to the person who in 1968 had inquired, "What is the Southwest Craft Center?" broke into a song of appreciation and rousing applause. It was, as McAllister stated, "a really big day in the life of the Southwest Craft Center." The following year the ceramics studio was named in honor of Edith McAllister, and Club Giraud opened to its members to begin generating financial support for the Craft Center.[27]

Praise Be the Volunteer

In January 1981, the same month that the concept of Club Giraud was proposed, the Southwest Craft Center formally acknowledged the invaluable role of its volunteers. The Craft Center had been built through the hard work and dedication of volunteers whose role had grown together with the organization. When the center moved to the Ursuline campus in 1971, its purpose expanded beyond the arts and education to embrace the preservation of its historic home. Accordingly, the volunteers redoubled their efforts to support this dual purpose through both staffing and fundraising. They hosted galas and parties to celebrate Christmas and San Antonio's annual Fiesta River Parade, staged art auctions, and established the successful annual arts fair. They staffed the sales gallery, cooked and served meals in the Copper Kitchen, and planted and pruned the gardens. Above all they were tireless and undeterred by challenges. Vieve Duncan, a generous donor to the center who chaired the Copper Kitchen volunteers and then the garden committee, exemplified the group's dedication. When the landscaping they had so carefully cultivated froze to the ground during one of San Antonio's few harsh winters, Duncan simply pruned the treasured avocado and bay trees and wrote to the members, "spring's just around the corner!"[28]

Now more tourists were discovering the Southwest Craft Center and its charming buildings, and Craft Center board member Harriet Ross proposed establishing a formal volunteer program. The program would be based in a new visitors' center, located in the old wood-working studio built originally as the Ursuline convent's first chapel. The Wood Room, as it had been called, was renamed La Sala and furnished with the altar, candlesticks, and other items from the convent's chapel. At the Craft Center's annual meeting on May 21, 1981, the room was dedicated to Emily Edwards, who had died the previous year.[29]

Like her aunt, Emily Edwards, Floy Fontaine Jordan was devoted to historic preservation and had a special fondness for the old Ursuline convent. In late 1982 Jordan donated funds to assure that the Emily Edwards Room would be properly outfitted for small exhibits, lectures, and meetings. As chairman of volunteers, Harriet Ross was given the challenging task of finding the person who would schedule programming for the room. Upon locating a willing and able volunteer, she was ecstatic. "Praise be," she wrote, "An angel by the name of Ethel Wheeler has agreed to be the Emily Edwards Room chairman. She is busily making lists of possible speakers, workshops, shows, etc. If you have a rip snorting idea, give her a call."[30] Ethel Wheeler and her volunteers subsequently developed a successful series of small exhibits and noontime lectures that attracted visitors to the Southwest Craft Center and educated them on topics related to the school's purpose.

Floy Edwards Fontaine (left) and her sister Emily Edwards sit among the ruins of the Ursuline Academy following the 1967 fire that destroyed the 1910 portion of the old school. *Southwest School of Art and Craft.*

A Living Legacy

While supervising renovation of the Emily Edwards Room in the early months of 1983, Ruth Johnson undertook another project— completion of the adjoining space to the east beyond a graceful limestone arch. Shortly before the Emily Edwards Room reopened in October 1983 and while the remainder of the small building was still being renovated, friends gathered to celebrate Amy Shelton McNutt's ninety-fourth birthday on August 23, 1983.[31] The occasion was highlighted by the announcement that McNutt's generosity would provide for completion of the space adjoining the Emily Edwards Room and an endowment for ongoing care of the Craft Center's grounds. Less than two months later, Amy Shelton McNutt died on October 14, 1983, knowing that the gardens she so loved would be maintained for the enjoyment of future generations. To recognize McNutt's outstanding contributions to the Southwest Craft Center, the room that had been completed with her last bequest was named the Amy Shelton McNutt Garden Room in her honor on April 7, 1987.[32]

Quality Above All Else

By mid-1983 the Southwest Craft Center's projected revenues, derived from diverse sources including tuition and gallery sales, had grown to $850,000, a two-fold increase in four years.[33] Director Darrell Bohlsen had reorganized the school's classes into five departments with 22 full-time and 6 part-time staff and [32] part-time instructors. Each department, with the exception of fine arts, had a full-time chairperson—Claire Holliday in metals, Dennis Smith in clay, Kay Maxham in fibers, and John McConkey in photography. The mortgage had been paid off, the new ceramics studio had been completed, and Club Giraud had opened. The Copper Kitchen lunchroom continued to attract downtown workers, and the lushly landscaped gardens, picturesque river landing, and charming Gothic Revival chapel had become favorite venues for tourists and for special-events rentals.

When Darrell Bohlsen left the Southwest Craft Center in June 1983 to pursue other interests, a search firm was retained to identify potential directors with both administrative skills and artistic sensitivities.[34] The organization was at a critical juncture in its growth and needed the right person to assure that it maintained its edge as a reputable and progressive arts institution. During the search the board sought programming advice from Jeffrey Moore, director of the

Top: Dennis Smith arrived at the school in 1976 as an assistant potter and subsequently became chair of the Ceramics Department. As the Southwest School of Art and Craft's longest-tenured instructor, Smith celebrated his 25th anniversary in 2001. *Southwest School of Art and Craft.*

Above: Beck Whitehead teaches a student in the Paper and Book Arts Department which she has chaired since 1989. *Southwest School of Art and Craft.*

Anderson Ranch Arts Center in Aspen, Colorado. "At the time, I didn't know they were looking for a director, and was thinking about devoting myself to painting full time." Moore was impressed by the Craft Center's preservation of the historic Ursuline site and its potential for earned income and enhanced programming. "I had the opportunity to develop a program on a much larger scale than what we had in Aspen. It was an opportunity I couldn't turn down." After a six-month search, Jeffery Moore was introduced as the center's incoming executive director in January 1984.

Moore's hiring signaled a renewed commitment on the part of the organization to achieve artistic excellence and recognition on a national level. In pursuit of that goal and stressing quality above all else, Moore built on the Craft Center's past accomplishments. He broadened programming to include an ambitious schedule of workshops by recognized artists and a strong artist-in-residence program. Before Moore completed his first year, the Craft Center had offered workshops by nationally prominent artists, including ceramists Ruth Duckworth, Ken Ferguson, and Jim Romberg, photographer Ernst Haas, papermaker/printmaker Helen Frederick, and fiber artist Walter Nottingham. Moore was candid: "We may not be making a lot of money off the workshops, but I think it is important for students to be exposed to working, professional artists."

Jeffrey Moore believed that the Southwest Craft Center's non-accredited status allowed it to remain flexible and creative in both programming and student mix. While some students were hobbyists, others were professionals, honing their skills and experimenting with new techniques. This dynamic environment was further stimulated by the relationship of students with local artists-in-residence who used the center's studios and taught classes. All of this fit well with Moore's philosophy. "I want beginners working with professionals in a classroom situation. I want people to know the difference between exhibiting quality professional work and craft fair work." [35]

As both an artist and an administrator, Moore also felt strongly that board members, as policy makers, must be knowledgeable about the school's artists and programs. He announced, "we'll spend some time talking about art."[36] Soon, faculty members and visiting artists were discussing their work at board meetings and were being entertained at receptions in board members' homes.

A Toast to Twenty Years

In February 1985, as the Southwest Craft Center's twentieth anniversary approached, board members reluctantly voted to close the La Villita gallery where their founding dream had first been realized in 1968. The gallery held many fond memories, and the board had struggled with this decision for almost three years.[37] The building lease was up for renewal, and because the city had completely renovated La Villita in 1981 and 1982, a rent increase was inevitable. Whereas the La Villita gallery once showcased fine crafts, these were now sold at the Ursuline, and the old shop stocked more easily marketed items. Reflective of the pragmatism that had brought the Craft Center to this point, it was Helen Marie Hendrie who, after summarizing the history of the La Villita gallery, concluded that it no longer fulfilled the Craft Center's purpose. It was agreed that other new programs could replace the gallery's revenue, and members voted to consolidate their gallery at the fully renovated Ursuline site.[38]

Two months later, in May 1985, members marked the twentieth anniversary of the Southwest Craft Center's founding. They invited Dr. Rhoderick Key, dean of Fine Arts at the University of Texas at San Antonio, to discuss "The Place of Art in Everyday Living." It was a subject that they understood very well. Many of them had devoted a great part of their lives for the past two decades to realizing the dream of the Southwest Craft Center. It was a journey that had taken them from historic La Villita to the Ursuline Academy. When Dr. Key concluded, they raised their champagne flutes in a toast to past and future accomplishments and cut a cake shaped like the landmark Ursuline clock tower.[39]

An Organization Comes of Age

Jeffrey Moore initiated new programs, scrutinized old ones, and expanded the most popular ones to maximize enrollment. A new graphics department and papermaking studio attracted a broader range of artists to the Southwest Craft Center, and additional looms allowed the successful weaving program to expand. Nationally recognized artists including designer Jack Lenor Larsen, photographer William

Wegman and ceramist Don Reitz continued to draw students and enhance the school's teaching program.

Beyond the center's control, however, was the economic crisis of the middle 1980s, brought about by the collapse of domestic oil prices. Texas was particularly hard hit, and the Craft Center was not alone among San Antonio's non-profit organizations that felt the impact. By August 1986 the center's earned income, memberships, and donations had all declined.[40]

Fortunately, generous gifts were made that supplemented the operating budget and precluded drastic cutbacks. Still, programs were carefully scrutinized for both their artistic content and earned income potential, and all expenditures were carefully monitored.[41] In the course of this austerity, the Southwest Craft Center became a more tightly run and professionally managed organization. In March 1987 the Texas Arts Alliance and Texas Commission on the Arts recognized the Southwest Craft Center as the state's best artistic organization in the education category.[42]

When Jeffrey Moore left the Craft Center after three years in 1987, founding trustees Maggie Block and Helen Marie Hendrie, who had provided continuity to the organization throughout its history, were charged with the search for his replacement.[43] Block and Hendrie were guided by the momentum of a successful program as well as by Jeffrey Moore himself. Moore, who valued the organization and understood its strengths and weaknesses, remained for an interim period and authored a report summarizing his thinking and hopes for the Craft Center's future. In it he underscored the center's accomplishments in its 22-year history, citing growth and success. "If the next Director is provided a professional structure from which to build, the Southwest Craft Center will take the next step towards continued growth and increased benefit to the community of San Antonio."[44]

Moore's report was both well received and supported by President Ann Thomas. The board subsequently revised its bylaws, making changes that included term limits to keep the organization fresh and flexible and the establishment of an artists' advisory committee. Moore, who assisted with the search for his successor, remarked, "the next person will have to come in very strong." On October 15, 1987, Jeffrey Moore's final day, the board welcomed Ric Collier as the new director.[45]

Houston metalsmith Sandra Zilker works in the new Willson Metals Studio during a 1999 workshop. *Southwest School of Art and Craft.*

A New Vision

Ric Collier had directed the Art Museum of South Texas in Corpus Christi for six years before coming to San Antonio. With a master's degree in sculpture and drawing and 12 years of experience in art administration, Collier was known among his peers as an innovative manager.[46] He was attuned to the school's faculty and programming and accustomed to working with board members to educate them about the arts. Looking to the future, Collier set out to strengthen the Southwest Craft Center's existing programs and to introduce new ones.

Collier spent much of his first two years grappling with the ongoing deficit resulting, at least in part, from the Texas recession. He looked for ways to broaden the center's audience and base of support and proposed a multi-disciplinary arts program that included not only the visual arts but also music, dance, theater, and literature.[47] Collier also sought to attract more visitors through both the center's exhibition and visiting artist program. An exhibit of quilts by Faith Ringgold, an installation by Jun Kaneko, and workshops by photographers Michael Kenna, paper maker Nance O'Banion, and ceramist Bennett Bean all highlighted the late 1980s and early 1990s.

Like his predecessor, Jeffrey Moore, Ric Collier also recognized the need for expansion of the physical facility. "I think my board is ready for some sort of major expansion. We need more space for more heavy, industrial kinds of crafts. We have this wonderful historic facility which generates revenue for us, but it limits us on the kinds of craft programs we can have." Collier dreamed of a "craft factory" where more industrial crafts, such as glass and welding, could be practiced. Like Moore, Collier stressed quality. "Whether it's art or craft, the thing that really matters is whether or not it's good design." [48]

Though charming and suited to certain Southwest Craft Center programs, the historic Ursuline buildings were fragile and not easily adapted to certain artistic processes. The structures had met all of the Craft Center's needs since 1970, but now the school had outgrown them. When Jeffrey Moore reported in January 1986 that the center had reached its physical capacity, a committee was appointed to explore purchase of the nearby Sears automotive building—a

Sears closed its downtown San Antonio facility in 1986, and in 1994 the store's old automotive building was purchased for conversion into studios and exhibition space for the Southwest School of Art and Craft. *Southwest School of Art and Craft.*

nondescript, modern structure that could be easily converted to new uses.

Sears had opened its store across from the Ursuline Academy in 1937 and constructed its automotive department in the 1950s at the corner of Navarro and Augusta streets, just north of the Ursuline property.[49] Ironically, in the post-war boom of the 1950s, Sears had considered acquiring the old Ursuline Academy grounds for parking, but now the tables were turned. Just as the sisters had abandoned their historic buildings to move to the suburbs, Sears built branch stores in new, outlying shopping malls. By the early 1980s Sears' flagship downtown store had fallen victim to suburban flight and the changing retail market.

The entire five-acre site was put up for sale in 1983, only shortly before Jeffrey Moore arrived at the Craft Center, and was sold on a lease-back basis that same year to a group of real estate investors.[50] Moore envisioned the property as the solution to the center's space needs, and in February 1986 the center's representatives bid unsuccessfully to acquire it. Sears finally closed its doors in March 1986, and the building was left vacant.[51] When Jeffrey Moore left the Craft Center in October 1987, purchase of the Navarro Street property was another five years away.

Ric Collier maintained Moore's vision of an expanded campus from his first days at the Southwest Craft Center. He toured the Sears automotive building in June 1988, and when the property was taken over by the Resolution Trust Corporation Craft Center representatives again began to negotiate. Again, they were unable to reach an agreement.[52] In May 1993, however, the board finally announced that the Southwest Craft Center had succeeded in purchasing the Navarro Street property and could begin planning for its future expansion.[53]

Planning for the Future; Preserving the Past

The Southwest Craft Center not only survived the economic crisis of the 1980s, but actually reaped its benefits with the purchase of the Sears building. Now, after more than seven years, the dream of an expanded site that would provide modern studios and spacious exhibition galleries was nearly a reality. Reinvigorated by these successes, the board selected founding members Edith McAllister and Maggie Block to co-chair the first public capital campaign in the center's history. McAllister and Block, who had each committed a quarter of a century to the Craft Center, set out to raise $3.5 million to renovate the newly acquired Navarro Campus, calling the effort the "Campaign for the Future to Preserve the Past."[54]

The new facility was planned to maximize flexible programming space and minimize detrimental use of the historic Ursuline buildings. When final space-allocation decisions were made, it was perhaps for both practical and sentimental reasons that the first programs to operate at the Ursuline Campus remained there. The fibers department and the Young Artist Programs, including the center's first and still successful educational effort, Saturday Morning Discovery, remained in the historic stone structures where they had been since that first cold winter of 1971. The nearby ceramics studio, completed in 1982, also remained within the confines of the old convent wall. Across Navarro Street the new facility would house expanded exhibition galleries and studios for the metals, papermaking, photography, and surface design departments.

The $3.5 million capital campaign strained the Southwest Craft Center's operating budget, and though half of the funds were raised by January 1995 cuts in non-essential expenses were still required.[55] The board successfully weathered this defining and stressful time as it had in the past, by reaffirming its commitment to the center's founding purpose as a teaching institution. When Ric Collier left the directorship in January 1996, this commitment guided members as they searched for his replacement.[56]

Preparing for the New Millennium

At the conclusion of a six-month search, Paula Berg Owen, director of the Hand Workshop Art Center in Richmond, Virginia, was selected to lead the Southwest Craft Center. Owen had spent 11 years at the Hand Workshop developing it into a regional cultural institution with a respected reputation. In Richmond, stressing community accessibility and involvement, Owen had succeeded in greatly expanding the workshop's facilities as well as its programming and fund raising capabilities.[57] Now she would assist the Craft Center in completing its ambitious capital campaign and campus expansion.

Owen assumed the directorship of an organization that was operating in the black for the first time in many years. In June, shortly before she arrived, the board heard the positive news that "the Craft Center has done an amazing turn-around from where we were at this same time last year."[58] At her first meeting on August 27, 1996, Owen was able to report that the organization was debt free and had a healthy year-end surplus. In September, however, Owen outlined certain internal conditions and needs that required attention and resources to assure a successful expansion to the Navarro Campus. To achieve this transition she recommended a complete strategic planning process, and for the remainder of 1996 the organization worked to develop this document. The resulting three-year plan presented in January 1997 integrated all aspects of the institution with its ambitious growth plan into the year 2000.

The 1997 strategic plan was based on the premises of quality and professionalism in both administration and programming. It also reaffirmed long standing goals—national recognition, the preservation of the site's history and historic buildings, and the center's standing as an important community resource. The plan included many critical elements—the building of administrative systems and infrastructure, a strong working relationship between board and staff, an expanded

Southwest School of Art and Craft board members gathered to study plans to convert the Sears automotive center into the school's new Navarro Campus. *(left to right: Adelle Brewer, Andres Andujar, Bernard Lifshutz, Edith McAllister, Maggie Block, Bob Dickemper, and Mike Lance). Southwest School of Art and Craft.*

artistic program including painting, drawing, and interdisciplinary curricula, presentation of exhibitions that were integrated with the studio program, and a broad and diverse staff, student body, and audience. In 1997 the board and staff set out to fulfill this ambitious blueprint for the short-term future.

Five years elapsed between the planning and the construction of the Navarro Campus. When the when bids were received the lowest exceeded projections by $350,000. The board remained committed to the project and voted in September 1997 to proceed in spite of the increased cost. Drawing on two decades of experience, Maggie Block addressed her colleagues, noting that this was not the first time the Craft Center founders or trustees were faced with a fiscal challenge. After 25-plus years of successful fundraising, Block expressed faith in the San Antonio community's belief and affection for the Craft Center.[59] As before, Block's faith was affirmed.

Financial stability and identity were integral to the Southwest Craft Center's strategic plan as well as its ongoing success.

Addressing these issues and looking forward to the organization's future in the new millennium, two ambitious steps were taken in December 1997. First, a campaign called Fund 2000 was initiated to raise an additional $2.5 million to complete the Navarro Campus, continue renovation of the historic Ursuline buildings, and supplement the center's endowment fund. Second, and perhaps just as important, was the reexamination of the Southwest Craft Center's name, the foremost public expression of its identity in the community.

What's in a Name?

There had been inconclusive proposals to change the Southwest Craft Center's name in previous years, but after Paula Owen's arrival she carefully analyzed the center's identity and was amazed at the number of people who thought highly of the Craft Center but did not know what it did, or why.[60]

Understanding that a clear identity was needed for effective marketing, she proposed the name change. The nuance in meaning between "Southwest Craft Center" and "Southwest School of Art and Craft" not only clarified the school's program but also acknowledged an evolutionary trend. By the late twentieth century, the concept of crafts had evolved from embracing only traditionally functional objects to including contemporary art objects created using traditional techniques. The distinct line between art and craft that had once been clearly drawn was now, in reality, blurred.

From the time of its founding, the center had offered classes in both crafts and various fine arts media. Early in its history the center's teaching program had been called the "Creative Arts School," but the term had slipped from usage after being removed from the center's letterhead. Paula Owen wanted the public to clearly understand that the center was indeed a school, and that art and craft were increasingly intertwined. She and board chair Adelle Brewer presented the case to the board in October 1997, citing the change as a business strategy. "Southwest" placed the school as the region's only professional level, non-degree granting art school. "School" was nomenclature that implied a seriousness and quality of purpose. First-tier American art and craft teaching facilities, Owen noted, were "schools" not "centers."

Southwest School of Art and Craft director Paula Owen, board chairman Adelle Brewer, and City Councilman Roger Flores II unveiled the school's new name on June 2, 1998. *Southwest School of Art and Craft.*

"Art and craft" implied the interrelationship of disciplines inherent in the school's curriculum.

To many this might have seemed a small change, but in actuality the new name reaffirmed the founding purpose of the school. Through the hard work of countless dedicated individuals over the course of almost 30 years, the Southwest Craft Center had developed from simply a concept, formalized in articles of incorporation, into a multi-faceted, multi-million dollar organization. No one understood and appreciated this more than those who had provided continuity to the Craft Center throughout its history. When the name change motion was formally presented to the board in December 1997, it was seconded by Margaret Willson, who had invited interested supporters to her home in 1963 to discuss founding the organization.[61]

May the Transformation Continue

"Transformation" was the theme aptly selected to celebrate the new name and the new facility dubbed the Navarro Campus of the Southwest School of Art and Craft. It was a theme inherent in the school's strategic plan that envisioned maximizing new opportunities presented by the Navarro Campus while retaining the vibrancy of the Ursuline Campus. Twenty-seven years had elapsed since the school

"Transformation" was the theme of the celebration that marked the grand opening of the school's new Navarro Campus on September 27, 1998. *Southwest School of Art and Craft.*

moved from two small buildings in La Villita to the old Ursuline convent. Renovation of the dilapidated buildings was nearly complete, and the new 33,000-square-foot Navarro Campus offered opportunities undreamed of on that first cold day of classes in January 1971. On September 26 and 27, 1998, board members, supporters, craftsmen, artists, and the community at large gathered to celebrate these accomplishments. When the old Sears automotive store re-opened to the public as the Navarro Campus of the Southwest School of Art and Craft on a hot September Sunday, the San Antonio *Express-News* editorialized, "May the transformation continue."[62]

One year later it was apparent that the transformation was well underway. With the opening of the Navarro Campus, the school had doubled its enrollment capacity and quadrupled its exhibition space. The new campus provided facilities for exhibitions and gallery talks that expanded the school's regional visibility and capability to target new audiences. The new Russell Hill Rogers Gallery was inaugurated with an impressive exhibition titled "Transformations" that included works by 24 San Antonio artists. Within a year of its opening, the gallery was the site of nationally recognized exhibitions, including "The Potters of Mata Ortiz: Transforming a Tradition." For the first time in its history, the school was able to present large exhibitions in a museum-quality setting accompanied by interpretive programming.

The Russell Hill Rogers Gallery at the Navarro Campus expanded the Southwest School of Art and Craft's exhibition space and enabled the school to host nationally recognized exhibitions such as, "The Potters of Mata Ortiz: Transforming a Tradition." *Southwest School of Art and Craft.*

It was also possible at the new campus to add book arts, design, drawing and painting, and printmaking classes to a curriculum that already included ceramics, photography, papermaking, weaving and fiber arts, surface design, and metalsmithing.[63] The staff now included 30 full-time people and hundreds of San Antonio's most accomplished artists and art educators. Among them were Jane Dunnewold, Carolina Flores, Sherry Fotopoulos, Phuong-Thao Hua, Robert Hils, Claire Holliday, Jim LaVilla-Havelin, Alberto Mijangos, Regina Sanders, Alberto Saucedo, Dennis Smith, Tim Summa, and Beck Whitehead.

The Visiting Artist Program had continued to bring gifted artists to San Antonio. In the late 1990s potter Shinman Yamada of Okinawa, weaver Jason Collingwood from England, Els van Baarle of the Netherlands, porcelain artist Cho Ki Jung of Korea, and Vicki and Pablo Sigwald of Argentina, all international artists of note, joined the 25 United States artists who taught at the school.

Volunteers and staff could be justifiably proud of the results of their hard work and careful planning at the close of 1999. The institution's budget remained in the black, and in the past three school terms approximately 2,000 adults and 1,600 children had enrolled on-campus, a 20% increase since 1997, and another 10,000 children had participated in Young Artist Programs off-campus in schools, community

Artists Therese Zemlin and Tom Lagagnina exhibited their works in the show "Abstract Craft: The Non-Objective Object." *Southwest School of Art and Craft.*

centers, and shelters. Final renovations were underway at the Ursuline Campus, and planning had already begun for the next celebration.

The Southwest School of Art and Craft's mission statement was twofold, stating its role both as a place for teaching, exhibition, and appreciation of art and as well as a place of historic significance. The strategic plan for 2000-2003 acknowledged this dual purpose and emphasized, as one of its goals, increased attention to the school's historical importance. In fulfillment of this goal, long time trustee and volunteer Ellie Lamb, assisted by numerous volunteers and donors, collected, catalogued, and assured proper storage for archival materials—the earliest from the nineteenth century—that documented the rich history of the buildings and the school.[64] The Southwest School of Art and Craft Archives was given a spacious and appropriate home when the metals department moved from the second floor of the dormitory to the Navarro Campus. To complement the archives and make this history tangible, a Visitors Center Museum was envisioned to tell the long and important story of the site and school. Finally, to commemorate its past at the beginning of a new millennium, the Southwest School of Art and Craft paused in September 2001 to remember the Ursuline sisters' arrival there and to celebrate 150 years of education within the historic stone walls.

September: The Month of Transformations

The transformation of the site had truly begun on September 20, 1840, when a newly arrived Catholic missionary, Father Jean Marie Odin, envisioned a school for girls rising from the frontier and purchased 12 wild acres on the meandering San Antonio River. Odin kept this dream alive during his missionary years and in September 1848, as a bishop, made his final decision to build the school. Eleven years elapsed between the time Odin first observed the site and the Ursuline sisters arrived on September 14, 1851, to establish the school. From the first day of classes until the Ursuline sisters sold the academy site 114 years later on September 1, 1965, the buildings witnessed the education of thousands of young girls. After only a five-year hiatus, the Southwest Craft Center convened Saturday Morning Discovery classes, and Kay Maxham began to instruct two students in the art of weaving at the old Ursuline. No other place in San Antonio had enjoyed such a long and distinguished association with the art of learning.

Approaching the 150th anniversary of the first classes held by the Ursuline sisters at this historic site, the Southwest School of Art and Craft remained steadfastly committed to setting a firm course in the new millennium. The board recognized that the new Navarro Campus symbolized the next chapter in the history of both the school and Ursuline site, and that it was their responsibility to assure this ongoing educational legacy. With the same commitment that, in only 35 years, had transformed the organization into a $2.5 million operation attracting 250,000 participants and visitors annually, the Southwest School of Art and Craft's original founders again guided the board as it successfully raised $2.5 million to complete Fund 2000. This accomplishment assured that the school's studios would be fully finished, historic renovations would be completed, and operating endowments would be established.

As the Southwest School of Art and Craft prepared to celebrate the sesquicentennial of its historic site, Maggie Block's words expressed almost 20 years earlier still rang true. Thanking the thousands of volunteers who had brought the organization so far she said, "Looking back I am overwhelmed anew at the tremendous outpouring of generosity and support which have made the Craft Center. The staggering amounts of time and interest given by members, artists, and craftsmen,

Opposite Top: Potter Shinman Yamada of Okinawa was among the visiting artists of international note who taught at the Southwest School of Art and Craft in the late 1990s and later. *Southwest School of Art and Craft.*

Opposite Far Left: Tiles produced in 1998 by visiting artist Angelica Pozo in collaboration with the school's advanced ceramics class were installed by ceramics studio assistant, Diana Kersey, and Ceramics Department chairman Dennis Smith. *Southwest School of Art and Craft.*

Opposite Right: Visiting artist David MacDonald demonstrated surface treatments for a clay vessel during his 1998 workshop. *Southwest School of Art and Craft.*

the creative thinking, the helping hands, the display cases, air conditioners, old sinks and new equipment, buckets of clay, a barrel of shoe laces, bushels of yarn, invaluable advice, help—legal, accounting, copying—gallons of paint, old furniture and a load of firewood, friends to help lighten the task and clear the path. The list is endless, as is our appreciation and gratitude. As I look at what the Craft Center is today, I hope that all those who helped so much are as proud as I am!"[65]

The Southwest School of Art and Craft is indeed a magnificent tribute to a 150-year legacy that began inauspiciously among weeds and debris on a moonlit night in 1851. When observers reflects on the past century and a half, they can see the rise of sturdy buildings along the San Antonio River, witness the evolution of the city's first Catholic school for girls, share the challenges faced by the strongest of San Antonio's preservationists, and admire years of unselfish commitment on the part of countless volunteers who labored to elevate the role of art and craft in the community and perpetuate the educational tradition of this unique and tranquil place. This transformation has been achieved by a disparate group of people, separated by time, background, and motivation, all of whom helped to shape, and were in turn shaped by, this place.

The Southwest School of Art and Craft is the sum of this 150-year legacy. It is the inheritance of a new generation of stewards who will assure, with equal dedication and caring, that this place continues to serve the community in a new millennium.

Southwest School of Art and Craft students worked in the school's garden in the late 1970s. *Southwest School of Art and Craft.*

Notes

Ursuline art students gathered for class in the 1880s. *Institute of Texan Cultures, courtesy of Bill Cotulla.*

1 SWCC Board Minutes, June 6, 1975, SSAC.

2 Block to William Brown, January 12, 1976, SSAC. There is no record of a reply from Brown.

3 SWCC Board Minutes, September 27, 1978, SSAC.

4 SWCC *Newsletter* and "Scrapbooks" pertaining to the 1970s, SSAC.

5 The Ursuline Angel Committee to the Ursuline Angels, 1977-78, SSAC. "Meet the new Craft Center administrator," San Antonio *Express*, [March 1977].

6 SWCC Board Minutes April 4, 1978, SSAC; SWCC Executive Committee Minutes, March 7, 1978, SSAC.

7 Fiesta Week takes place during the week including April 21, the day marking the victory of the Texans over the Mexican Army at San Jacinto during the Texas Revolution.

8 SWCC Board Minutes, August 26, 1974, SSAC. The following year the Texas Folk Craft Experience was moved to July to avoid conflict with the Texas Folklife Festival, also held in August. In 1976 the event was renamed the Folk Craft Experience to distinguish it further from the Texas Folklife Festival.

9 SWCC Board Minutes, August 23, 1978, SSAC. The 1978 Folk Craft Experience raised $18,000 from admissions, activities, and advertising sales.

10 SWCC Board Minutes, September 27, 1978, SSAC; Russell, interview with the author, January 18, 2001, SSAC. Russell was also a volunteer with the Fiesta Commission, the oversight committee for the annual city-wide celebration that sponsored officially sanctioned Fiesta events during the annual April celebration.

11 Lunch rooms that benefited cultural groups were gaining popularity. At the time the Conservation Society, under the direction of Nancy Brown Negley, operated a lunch room at the José Antonio Navarro house. Whereas the Copper Kitchen has sustained itself for 25 years, the Conservation Society's effort was short lived.

12 "Garden dedication today," *North San Antonio Times*, June 6, 1975. The ironwork, given by John Holmgreen, owner of Alamo Iron Works, was from San Antonio's old Fourth Street Bridge that once spanned the river near the Ursuline Academy.

13 SWCC Board Minutes, July 11, 1978, SSAC. As garden chairman, Margaret Deeley had discussed the river landing with city officials in August 1975, but the project was delayed by lack of funding. Deeley also envisioned a garden between the convent wall and the river, but she saw only a simple, swept dirt garden under the pecan trees.

14 SWCC Board Minutes, March 7, 1979, SSAC. It was at this time that the Craft Center board retained outside accountants to assist with monthly financial statements in order to help manage its increasingly complex holdings. Personnel policies and procedures were also developed and an advisory committee of local businessmen was established.

15 SWCC Board Minutes, July 11, 1978, SSAC. "Mag" Tobin had donated use of a house on Eighth Street for the first Saturday Morning Discovery classes in 1969 and had worked actively with the Conservation Society in its efforts to acquire the Ursuline property. The committee also included Maggie Block, Edith McAllister, Evelyn Berg, Walter Mathis, and Jesse Oppenheimer.

16 SWCC Board Minutes, January 17, 1979, SSAC.

17 SWCC Board Minutes, May 2, 1979, SSAC.

18 SWCC Executive Committee Minutes, September 19, 1979, SSAC.

19 Block to Board Members, June 2, 1979, SSAC.

20 SWCC Board Minutes, February 25, 1981, SSAC.

21 SWCC Executive Committee Minutes, November 20, 1979, SSAC; SWCC Board Minutes, September 23, 1981, SSAC; Jacqueline Rather Beretta, telephone interview with the author, February 14, 2001. The two collections were Mary Austin Beretta's renowned dollhouses and miniatures and Bob Winn's extensive Mexican folk art holdings. Beretta's dollhouses and miniatures were eventually included in the collections of the Kansas City Dollhouse Museum and the Dallas Dollhouse Museum. The Winn Collection, administered by an advisory committee after his death in 1978, was donated to the San Antonio Museum of Art where, with the expansive Rockefeller Collection, it became part of one of the country's most impressive holdings of Latin American folk art. Following negotiations, the gift, described as "a good teaching tool as well as a tourist attraction," was approved on September 23, 1981. The local press announced on December 26, 1981 ("SWCC awarded art collection," San Antonio *Light*) that the Winn Collection had been given to the Southwest Craft Center and that a new folk art museum would open in the first academy building by the following Christmas. However, upon closer examination, the board decided that the administration and display of the collection would be too complicated because of limited space and staff (SWCC Board Minutes, September 22, 1982).

22 "Poof! It's all Craft Center now," San Antonio *Light*, February 16, 1981. At a special executive committee meeting on September 15, 1980, members discussed various measures to reduce the deficit, including paying off the parking lot note. The loan balance on December 1, 1980, was estimated at $124,574, after considering donations and pledges.

23 SWCC Board Minutes, January 28, 1981, SSAC. Maggie Block also credits David Straus as recommending formation of such a club (SWCC Newsletter, August-September-October 1981).

24 The Southwest Foundation for Research and Education is an internationally known science research center based in San Antonio."Quaint old Argyle Hotel restoration project set," San Antonio *Express*, July 10, 1955.

25 SWCC Board Minutes, September 23, 1981, SSAC. Lawyer Jesse Oppenheimer, who had drawn up the legal documents for the Argyle Club over twenty-five years earlier, assisted the Craft Center board in setting up Club Giraud.

26 "SWCC dedication honors McAllister," San Antonio *Express,* June 2, 1982.

27 SWCC Board Minutes, May 25, 1983, SSAC.

28 SWCC *Newsletter*, Winter 1981-82.

29 SWCC Board Minutes, January 28, 1981; March 25, 1981, SSAC; "SWCC to open Emily Edwards Room," San Antonio *Express-News*, May 17, 1981; "Emily Edwards Room honors 'very thorough woman,'" San Antonio *Express,* May 25, 1981.

30 Ross to SWCC Volunteers, August 10, 1983, SSAC.

31 Southwest Craft Center *Newsletter*, September 1983, SSAC.

32 SWCC Board Minutes, February 25, 1987, SSAC; Ross to Volunteers, [March 1987], SSAC; "Garden Room to bloom," San Antonio *Express-News*, April 7, 1987. The chapel's old altarpiece and other furnishings were moved from the Emily Edwards Room to the Amy Shelton McNutt Garden Room, where the work of Southwest Craft Center artists was also exhibited. After Jeffrey Moore became director of the Southwest Craft Center in March 1984, the Emily Edwards Room was re-named the Emily Edwards Gallery and became the site for one-person exhibits by the center's artist-instructors.

33 Bohlsen to Chrisman, April 25, 1983, SSAC.

34 SWCC Board Minutes August 31, 1983, SSAC.

35 "Quality is made here," San Antonio *Express-News*, December 28, 1984. In less than a year, the faculty increased from 12 to 35 instructors, and whereas fewer than 300 students were enrolled in fall 1983 classes, some 500 attended in fall 1984.

36 SWCC Board Minutes, March 28, 1984, SSAC.

37 SWCC Board Minutes, March 24, 1982, SSAC.

38 Ibid., February 27, 1985, SSAC.

39 Ibid., May 22, 1985, SSAC.

40 SWCC Board Minutes, August 27, 1986; December 17, 1986; SSAC.

41 Operation of the Copper Kitchen was an ongoing concern. In 11 years and under a series of managers, the restaurant had been an unpredictable revenue source.

With advice from Ron Given, manager of Club Giraud, the Craft Center's board hired Raymond Brown in 1987 to manage the Copper Kitchen.

42 "Craft center to receive arts award," San Antonio *Express-News*, April 1, 1987. The award was shared with the Houston Museum of Fine Arts.

43 "Craft Center forms search panel, " San Antonio *Light*, April 28, 1987.

44 "Director's Report," Southwest Craft Center, May 11, 1987, SSAC.

45 "Craft center in transition phase," San Antonio *Light*, June 14, 1987; SWCC Board Minutes, October 15, 1987, SSAC.

46 "Southwest Craft Center ends director search," San Antonio *Light*, October 3, 1987. Collier studied sculpture and drawing at Washington State University. He served two years as director of the Missoula Museum of Art, four years as director of the Boise Gallery of Art, and six and a half years as director of the Art Museum of South Texas.

47 SWCC Board Minutes, May 17, 1988, SSAC. Though a series of musical events proved popular, the dance, theater, and literature programs were never developed.

48 "Craft Center expansion is new director's goal," San Antonio *Express-News*, February 21, 1988.

49 "Romana Plaza new home of Sears store," San Antonio *Light*, April 18, 1937. Sears moved here from its previous site on the lower floors of the Smith-Young Tower. The Romana Plaza building had been constructed in 1929 to house the Maverick-Clarke Lithography Company.

50 "Downtown Sears store sold," San Antonio *Light*, June 24, 1983. The real estate consortium included a local savings and loan association.

51 "Soledad Sears closing Monday," San Antonio *Express-News*, March 27, 1986; SWCC Board Minutes, January 22, 1986; February 26, 1986; SSAC.

52 SWCC Board Minutes, May 17, 1988; June 21, 1988, SSAC. The Resolution Trust Corporation (RTC) was the agency formed to dispose of properties after the savings and loan association collapse of the late 1980s.

53 SWCC Board Minutes, October 27, 1992; April 27, 1993; May 18, 1993; March 29, 1994; SSAC. The site was separated into two parcels, a large tract where the main Sears store stood and the smaller tract with the automotive center. City Council approved acquisition of the larger parcel as the site of the new Central Library in February 1991. The RTC agreed to a price of $643,500 for the automotive center in October 1992, but the Craft Center's advisors urged the board to take a wait-and-see attitude. At an RTC auction seven months later, the center successfully bid $340,000, and the sale closed on March 11, 1994.

54 SWCC Board Minutes, March 29, 1994; September 23, 1997; SSAC. Betty Huth Coates, who had given generously to the Craft Center in honor of her mother and aunt, both Ursuline alumni, was the campaign's honorary chairman.

55 "Center half way to fund target," San Antonio *Express, Northeast Sun*, January 25, 1995. Among the cost cutting measures was suspension of the exhibition program that the board felt was increasingly expensive and often not related to the center's purpose.

56 "Southwest Craft Center chief Collier resigns amid $3.5 million funding drive," San Antonio *Express-News*, January 6, 1996. SWCC Board Minutes, January 23, 1996.

57 Richmond (Virginia) *Times-Dispatch*, May 28, 1996.

58 SWCC Board Minutes, June 25, 1996, SSAC.

59 SWCC Board Minutes, September 23, 1997, SSAC.

60 Owen to Cooper and Brewer, May 5, 1996, SSAC; "Director's Report," Southwest Craft Center, October 28, 1997, SSAC.

61 SWCC Board Minutes, December 9, 1997, SSAC.

62 "New name, new site to celebrate in S.A.," San Antonio *Express-News*, September 27, 1998.

63 After the San Antonio Art Institute closed, the McNay Museum became the owner of its fixtures and generously donated valuable printmaking equipment to the Southwest School of Art and Craft. The original press had been donated to the San Antonio Art Institute by Southwest School of Art and Craft founder Margaret Pace Willson.

64. This effort built on earlier work by volunteers Ann Goldsmith who researched the school's history and Francine Rowden who translated early French documents about the Ursuline Academy.

65. SWCC *Newsletter*, August 9, 1981.

Southwest School of Art and Craft founders Edith McAllister *(front)*, Helen Marie Hendrie, Maggie Block and Margaret Pace Willson *(from left)* gathered in 1991 to celebrate the school's Silver Anniversary. Founder Nancy Brown Negley is not pictured. *San Antonio Light*.

THE FOUNDERS:

AN ENDURING LEGACY

THE six individuals recognized as founders of the Southwest School of Art and Craft— Maggie Saunders Block, Helen Marie Hendrie, Edith McAllister, Nancy Brown Negley, Elizabeth (Betty) Urschel, and Margaret Pace Willson—each possessed different skills that combined to sustain the group through its early years when energy and creativity far exceeded tangible assets. They banded together to accomplish something new— the creation of an inclusive setting where artists working in different media could sell their work and thereby earn a living. Most notably, though the six women could have chosen more traditional ways to serve their community, they left comfortable suburban homes to spend their days transforming dilapidated inner-city buildings into an invaluable cultural asset. These individuals did not shy away from the often unglamorous and tedious tasks that were necessary to build an organization from the ground up. It was their commitment that inspired trust and confidence in potential donors, who were understandably skeptical of this ambitious and untested venture. Remarkably, four of the original six have remained active and devoted to the organization throughout its history. Betty Urschel died in 1988, and though Nancy Brown Negley moved away from San Antonio many years ago the Brown Foundation, founded by her family, has sustained its generosity that helped establish the school. Maggie Block, Helen Marie Hendrie, Edith McAllister, and Margaret Willson have continued to support the Southwest School of Art and Craft through their gifts of time, talent, and financial resources. Ever present and loyal, they have served as the institution's collective conscience and memory, remaining steadfast as staff and board members have come and gone through the years. Although the sesquicentennial celebration of the old Ursuline academy is a tribute to generations both past and present, special recognition is due the founders of the Southwest School of Art and Craft. They are the stewards who developed and preserved these treasured buildings to serve future generations both as a center of excellence in community education and as an urban retreat for all to enjoy.

The Southwest School of Art and Caft

Education was at the core of the Southwest Craft Center's purpose when it was organized in 1965. Founders stated that the new organization would "provide education in handcrafts" and seek to further and stimulate public interest in and appreciation of handcrafts and their use to enrich life and culture. After successfully opening a gallery in La Villita to showcase and sell the work of craftsmen from throughout the region, the board of the Southwest Craft Center turned to its educational mandate. One year after a Saturday morning program for young people began in February 1969, Craft Center members addressed the education of adults. They leased a second building, La Casita, near their gallery and asked noted local artists to teach workshops in ceramic sculpture, enameling, metal casting, weaving, macrame, stitching, batik, and hooking, and offered the classes at a modest fee. Soon, wood block printing, papier-mache, puppet making and woodcarving were added to the curriculum.

When the Southwest Craft Center moved its Creative Arts School to the old Ursuline Academy in late 1970, a more formal curriculum began to evolve. Before any renovation took place, weaver Kay Maxham set up looms at the center and taught her first two students there in October 1970. The following year, the fledgling ceramics program began when Bob Farmer, the center's first artist-in-residence, traded work for lodging and studio space and constructed a gas-fired kiln on the site. Photographer Tom Wright moved to the old Ursuline in 1972, built the center's first darkroom, and taught classes while supervising construction workers hired to renovate the old buildings. It was a time of creative quid pro quo when Craft Center volunteers and artists alike depended on one another as they simultaneously developed the school facilities and its curriculum.

Antecedents of many of the school's later programs were established in the 1970s and 1980s, when the center was struggling to achieve institutional stability, and the content and format of courses changed often. In 1979 Southwest Craft Center Director Darrell Bohlsen formally organized the school's classes into five departments—Fibers, Clay, Metals, Fine Arts, and Photography. These departments were later restructured and are now Fibers, Ceramics, Metals, Painting/ Drawing and Printmaking, Paper/Book Arts, Photography, and the Young Artist Programs.

Weaving, ceramics, and photography programs were popular from the school's earliest days at both La Villita and the old Ursuline. Kay Maxham directed the weaving program until shortly before her death in 1988 when the fibers program was named in her honor. She was succeeded by Robert Hils, who remains as department chair. When ceramic artist Bob Farmer left to work in Colorado with Paul Soldner, he was succeeded by Steve Humphrey and Bob Fromme. Fromme was joined by an assistant potter, Dennis Smith, who later became the school's longest tenured department chair. The photography work of Tom Wright was continued by Harvey Kohnitz, John McConkey, and Tim Summa. Victor Pagona is the current department chair.

The school offered its first book design classes in 1972, and 12 years later the Picante Paper Studio opened, made possible through the generosity of Margaret Pace Willson. The Paper and Book Arts Department, chaired by Beck Whitehead since 1989, remains one of the few facilities of its type in the United States.

Printmaking was among the first workshops presented in the late 1960s at La Casita, and a printmaking workshop was opened at the old Ursuline by Lee Newbury in 1976 funded by a grant from the Texas Commission on the Arts and Humanities. A silkscreening department was also established in the middle 1970s, and thought was given to establishing a graphics department as early as 1972. By 1976 graphics had become an established part of the curriculum. Related to all of these endeavors, Mary Vance Green and others discussed the need for a series of design workshops, and classes were introduced in 1974. Eva Templeton devoted ten years, from 1979 until 1989, to directing the Painting/Drawing and Printmaking Department that was reintroduced in 1999 and is chaired today by Margaret Craig.

Metals classes have evolved since the first enameling classes were held in 1968. Directed by John Rogers in its early years, the department has been chaired since 1979 by Claire Holliday. It now offers classes in basic skills, enameling, casting, and construction from the introductory to advanced levels.

The Surface Design Department was formally established in 1990 under the direction of Jane Dunnewold, who chaired the program until leaving the Southwest School of Art and Craft in 2000 to establish her own teaching and production studio. The department provided context to many of the school's popular but disparate classes. Courses in fabric and clothing design, drawing, painting, collage, calligraphy, and quilting, many of which had been offered at various times in the past, were now offered in a cohesive discipline. Since Dunnewold's departure the school has continued to teach many of these techniques through its Fibers Department.

The program of the Southwest School of Art and Craft has become more clearly delineated into four significant parts under the tenure of Director Paula Owen—the Adult Studio Program, the school's backbone since its founding; the Young Artist Programs, which have grown tremendously under the guidance of Director Jim LaVilla-Havelin; the Exhibition Program, which has expanded greatly with the opening of the 3,500-square foot Russell Hill Rogers Gallery at the Navarro Campus; and Public Programs, formalized in 2000 to include the Visitors' Center Museum, lectures, guest artist projects, and special events.

Today, as individuals of all ages enroll in classes, visitors tour the historic site, and the general public attends any of the diverse activities at the Southwest School of Art and Craft, it is clear to them that this is not simply a "school," but an institution of lifelong creative learning.

BIBLIOGRAPHY

Cited Works

Appler, Jules A. *General Directory and Blue Book* of the City of San Antonio, 1905-06. San Antonio: Jules A. Appler, [1906].

Burkhalter, Lois Wood. *Marion Koogler McNay: A Biography, 1883-1950.* San Antonio: Marion Koogler McNay Art Institute, 1968.

Castaneda, Carlos Eduardo. *Our Catholic Heritage in Texas, 1519-1936.* 7 vols. Austin: Von Boeckman-Jones, 1936.

Corner, William. *San Antonio de Bexar: A Guide and History.* San Antonio: Bainbridge and Corner, 1890.

Curtis, Albert. *Fabulous San Antonio.* San Antonio: Naylor, 1955.

Dinkins, Alfred George. *John Marie Odin, First Bishop of Texas.* Master's thesis, Trinity University, 1970.

Edwards, Emily. *Stones, Bells, Lighted Candles: Personal Memories of the Old Ursuline Academy in San Antonio at the Turn of the Century.* San Antonio: Daughters of the Republic of Texas Library, 1981.

Everett, Donald E. *Adobe Walls to Stone Edifice: A Sesquicentennial Pilgrimage of the First Presbyterian Church of San Antonio, Texas, 1846-1995.* San Antonio: First Presbyterian Church, 1995.

Fisher, Lewis F. *Crown Jewel of Texas: The Story of San Antonio's River.* San Antonio: Maverick, 1997.

Fisher, Lewis F. *Saving San Antonio: The Precarious Preservation of a Heritage.* Lubbock: Texas Tech University Press, 1996.

Gilbert, M.J., ed., *Archdiocese of San Antonio, Texas, 1874-1949.* San Antonio: Schneider Printing Company, 1949.

Henry, O. *The Complete Works of O.Henry.* Garden City, N.Y.: Garden City Publishing, 1937.

Herff, Ferdinand Peter. *The Doctors Herff: A Three-Generation Memoir.* San Antonio: Trinity University Press, 1973.

Heusinger, Edward W. *A Chronology of Events in San Antonio.* San Antonio: Standard, 1951.

Johnston, S.M. *Builders by the Sea: History of the Ursuline Community of Galveston, Texas.* New York: Exposition Press, 1971.

Lacey, Alice. *A Walk Through Old Ursuline into the Future.* San Antonio: Paul Anderson, 1986.

Letters from the Ursuline, 1852-1853. Edited by Catherine McDowell. San Antonio: Trinity University Press, 1977.

Morrison, Andrew. *The City of San Antonio.* St. Louis: Engelhardt, [1891].

Parisot, P.F., and C.J. Smith. *History of the Catholic Church in the Diocese of San Antonio, Texas.* San Antonio: Carrico and Bowen, 1897.

Red, William Stuart. *A History of the Presbyterian Church in Texas.* Austin: Steck Company, 1936.

Roemer, Ferdinand. *Texas: With Particular Reference to German Immigration and the Physical Appearance of the Country.* Translated by Oswald Mueller, 1935. Reprint. San Marcos: German-Texan Heritage Society, 1983.

1850 Census of Bexar County, Texas. Transcribed by Lauretta Russell. 1966. Reprint. San Antonio: San Antonio Genealogical and Historical Society, 1983.

Woolford, Bess Carroll, and Ellen Schulz Quillin. *The Story of the Witte Memorial Museum, 1922-1960.* San Antonio: San Antonio Museum Association, 1966.

Writers' Project of the Work Projects Administration in the State of Texas. *Old Villita.* San Antonio: Clegg Company, 1939.

Additional Reading

Crook, Cornelia English. *Henry Castro: A Study of Early Colonization in Texas.* San Antonio: St. Mary's Univeristy Press, 1988.

Domenech, Emmanuel. *Missionary Adventures in Texas and Mexico: A Personal Narrative of Six Years' Sojourn in Those Regions.* London: Longmans, Brown, Green, Longmans and Roberts, 1858.

Edwards, Emily. *F. Giraud and San Antonio: A Biography Based on Recorded Evidence Plus Circumstantial Surmises Based on this Evidence.* San Antonio: [Southwest Craft Center], 1979.

Goldsmith, Ann. "The History of the Southwest Craft Center." Typescript, Southwest School of Art and Craft, 1992.

Jordan, Floy Fontaine. *Foot-prints with Footnotes.* San Antonio: Floy Fontaine Jordan, 1991.

Kendall, Dorothy Steinbomer, and Carmen Perry. *Gentilz: Artist of the Old Southwest.* Austin: University of Texas Press, 1974.

Perrichon, Jean. *The Life of Bishop Dubuis, Apostle of Texas.* Lyons, France: Privately printed, 1900. Translated by Mme. Hectorine Piercey, 1978.

Sheridan, Mary Benignus. *Bishop Odin and the New Era of the Catholic Church in Texas, 1840-1860.* Ph.D. diss., St. Louis University, 1938.

Steinfeldt, Cecilia. *San Antonio Was: Seen Through a Magic Lantern.* San Antonio: San Antonio Museum Association, 1978.

Waugh, Julia Nott. *Castro-Ville and Henry Castro, Empresario.* 1934. Reprint. Austin: Nortex, 1986.

Weaver, Bobby D. *Castro's Colony: Empresario Development in Texas, 1842-1865.* College Station: Texas A&M University Press, 1985.

INDEX

Aberg, Charles, 78 n.33
Addams, Jane, 77 n. 23
Alamo (San Antonio de Valero), 8, 49
    n.12, 50nn. 23, 24, 27, 75 n. 4
Alamo Iron Works, 179 n. 12
Alexander, Kathleen, 125
Alvarez Bravo, Manuel, 77 n. 26
America House, 109 n. 18
American Craft Movement, 85
American Craftsmen's Cooperative
    Council, 85, 109 n. 18
American Craftsmen's Educational Council,
    109 n. 18
American Handcraft Council,109 n. 18
American Institute of Architects, 92
American Institute of Designers, 109 n. 16
Anderson Ranch Arts Center, 160
Andujar, Andres, 168
Angel Arches. *see under* Ursuline Academy
Angela Merici, Saint, 17, 46
Angels' Hall. *see under* Ursuline Academy
Appedole, W.J., 118, 121, 122, 138 n. 17
Argyle Club, 155, 180 n. 25
Arsenal, 75 n. 4
Art Jamboree, 110 n. 30
Art Museum of South Texas, 164
Art Weavers Guild, 82
Atwater, Mary Meigs, 107 n. 7

Baird, Arthur, 78 n. 36
Ballet Folklorico, 118, 119
Bean, Bennett, 164
Bennett, Eleanor, 138 n. 17
Bennett, John, 122, 138 n. 17
Beretta, Mary Austin, 179 n. 21
Berg, Evelyn, 123, 125, 134, 135, 179 n. 15
Berg, Tom, 125, 139 n. 21
Bible Society of New York, 9, 10
Big Craft Deal. *see under* Southwest School
    of Art and Craft
Black, Harding, 82, 107 n. 6, 111 n. 64
Blanc, Anthony (archbishop of New
    Orleans), 2, 8, 16, 18, 24
Block, Maggie Saunders, 89, 90, 94, 105,
    113, 116-121, 123, 125-128, 133, 134,
    136, 141, 144, 149, 150, 163, 166, 168,

175, 183, 184, 110 n. 43, 138 n. 17, 140
    n. 45, 179 n. 15, 180 n. 23
Blount, Beverly, 133, 134
Bohlsen, Darrell, 153, 155, 159, 186
Boise Gallery of Art, 181 n. 46
Bolner, Clifton, 55 n.126
Bonner, Mary, 108 n. 7
Borglum, Gutzon, 82, 108 n. 8
Brackenridge, George W., 108 n. 8
Bradley, David, 86
Brennan, Harold, 86
Brewer, Adelle, 168-170
Bristow, Bill, 142
Bristow, Wilanna, 97, 142
Brooks, Lois, 142
Brothers of Mary, 20
Brown Foundation, 89, 184, 110 nn. 37, 39,
    139 n. 27
Brown, George R., 110 n. 37
Brown, Raymond, 181 n. 41
Brown, William J., 141, 178 n. 2
Buffard, Fr. Etienne, 24, 26, 27
Burger, J., 24
Burnham, Douglas, 106
Butler, Glynn S., 68

Callaghan, Bryan, 13, 75 n. 8
Calvert, Richard, 138 n. 14
Campbell, David, 109 n. 23
Campbell, John, 31, 53 n. 88
Campbell, Kate, 20, 51 n. 58
Cantu, Clare O'Farrell, 125, 137
Carson, Chris, 136
Cassiano, José, 13
Castro, Henri, 6, 8, 50 n. 39
Castroville, 1, 7, 8, 18, 49 nn. 19, 21, 50 n.
    39
Celmins, Hagar, 105
Central High School, 31, 33
CETA (Comprehensive Employment
    Training Act), 123, 138 n. 20
Chamber of Commerce Tourist Attractions
    Committee, 92
Champagne Under the Stars. *see under*
    Southwest School of Art and Craft
Chen, Lucia, 97

Chicago Art Institute, 65, 77 n. 23, 108 n. 10

Chilhuly, Dale, 142

Choy, Katherine, 108 n. 14

Clarkson, Kate Campbell Merritt, 20

Club Giraud, 43, 99, 131, 155, 156, 159, 180 n. 25

Coates, Elizabeth (Betty) Huth, 125, 126, 134-137, 139 n. 22, 140 n. 44, 181 n. 54

Coates, George, 139 n. 22

Coliseum League, 38, 54 n. 110

Collier, Ric, 163-165, 167, 181 n. 46

Collingwood, Jason, 172

Collingwood, Peter, 160

Colonial Hills, 61, 63, 76 nn. 21, 22

Colquhoun, Ludovic, 4, 49 n. 14

Concepción Mission, 3, 5, 50 nn. 23, 39

Considerant, Victor, 50 n. 39

Copper Kitchen. *see under* Southwest School of Art and Craft

Coppini, Pompeo, 77 n. 23

Council House Fight, 3, 49 n. 9

Cowen, Link, 70, 72, 73, 118, 133

Craft Guild of San Antonio, 84-87, 105

Craft Horizons, 109 n. 18

Craig, Margaret, 187

Creative Arts School. *see under* Southwest School of Art and Craft

Culmer, Lessi Ellen Woolridge, 96, 109 n. 16

Cunningham, Joe, 101

Deeley, Margaret, 151, 179 n. 13

de la Garza, Rudecinda, 19, 20, 53 n. 85. *see also* Ursuline Sisters: Mary Magdalen, Mother

Del Alamo Urban Renewal Area, 74

Dickemper, Bob, 168

Dickinson, Stirling, 109 n. 16

Dielmann, Edna, 70

Dielmann, Henry, 70

Dillon, Kate, 31

Dobie, J. Frank, 60

Dotson, Tracy, 96, 97

Dozier, Velma, 100

Drossaerts, Arthur J. (archbishop of San Antonio), 44

Droste, Mary Elizabeth, 53 n. 82

Drought, Ethel Tunstall, 81, 82, 77 n. 32, 107 nn. 4, 5

Drought, H.P., 107 n. 4

Droughtfels, 107 n. 4

Dubose, Rena, 85, 98

Dubuis, Claude Marie (bishop of Galveston), 1, 2, 6-8, 18, 19, 22-24, 26, 27, 61, 49 n. 21

Duckworth, Ruth, 160

Duderstadt, Bruce, 97, 105

Duncan, Baker, 155

Duncan, Vieve, 157

Dunnewold, Jane, 172, 187

Dwyer, Edward, 13

Ebendorf, Bob, 142

Ecole Centrale des Arts et Manufactureres (Paris), 12

Ecole des Arts et Métiers (Chalon, France), 13

EDA (Economic Development Administration), 133, 134, 151, 140 n. 42

Edwards, Emily, 33, 63-66, 68, 136, 157, 158, 75 n. 9, 77 nn. 23, 26, 32

Edwards, Helen, 59, 63, 64

Edwards, Lillian, 63, 64

Entienne, Rosalie. *see under* Ursuline Sisters: St. Isidore

Espada Mission, 3

Ewing Halsell Foundation, 139 n. 27

Farmer, Bob (potter), 117, 128, 130, 185, 186, 139 n. 26

Farmer, Bob (EDA), 134

Fenstermaker, Martha, 100, 101, 128, 132, 139 n. 24

Ferguson, Ken, 160

Fiesta Arts Fair. *see under* Southwest School of Art and Craft

Fiesta Commission, 144, 178 n. 10

Flores, Carolina, 172

Flores, Roger, II, 170

Folk Craft Experience. *see under* Southwest School of Art and Craft

Fontaine, Floy Edwards, 59, 64, 158

Ford, O'Neil, 60, 75 n. 11

Ford, Powell, and Carson, 76 n. 11

Ford, Wanda Graham, 58, 60, 138 n. 2

Fotopoulos, Sherry, 172

Fourth Street Bridge, 179 n. 12

Fox Tech High School, 53 n. 95

Frazer, Robert, 111 n. 51

Frederick Douglass School, 53 n. 94

Frederick, Helen, 160

Frey, Berta, 107 n. 7

Fromme, Bob, 142, 186

Frost Brothers, 96, 99, 109 n. 16

Frost, Adele, 134, 151, 140 n. 41
Frost, Jack, 151

Gaenslen, F. B. 40, 41, 54 n. 112
Gallagher Ranch, 148, 150
Gallagher, Terry, 106
Galt, Gloria, 98, 110 n. 32
Gentilz, Marie, 24
Gentilz, Theodore, 107 n. 1
German English School, 28
Gevinson, Daniel, 66, 68, 69, 77 nn. 27, 31,
    78 n. 36
Girard, Alexander, 86
Giraud, François, 10-16, 18, 20, 27, 66,
    156, 50 nn. 32, 33, 51 n. 49, 52 n. 75,
    53 n. 88
Giraud, Theodore, 10, 12, 50 n. 33
Given, Ron, 181 n. 41
Goldsmith, Ann, 182 n. 64
Golla, Emil, 94
Gonzales, Boyer, 82, 108 n. 8
Goodall, Donald B., 109 n. 23
Graham, Elizabeth, 75 n. 2
Greco, Dominic, 106
Green Pastures, 57
Green, Mary Vance, 82, 86, 87, 89, 97, 100,
    101, 105, 116, 187, 110 n. 36, 139 n. 24
Green, Rena Maverick, 77 n. 23, 139 n. 24
Greenwood, Marianne, 138 n. 9
Gregory XVI, 2
Griffith, Jean (Mrs. Walter C.), 107 n. 7
Grotto, Lady of Lourdes. see under Ursuline
    Academy
Guenther, Jack, 89
Guerra, Henry, Jr., 76 n. 17
Guilbeau, François, 13, 58, 50 n. 40
Guilbeau, François, House, 58, 59, 50 n. 40,
    75 nn. 3, 4
Guzmán, Luis, 142, 156

Haas, Ernst, 160
Hagy, Virgil, 96, 101
Hallman, Ted, 142
Hamlin, Vivian, 115
Hammond, Pat, 145
Hancock, Kitty, 100
Hand Workshop Art Center, 167
Handcraft Cooperative League of America,
    109 n. 18
Harlow, Diane Hendrie. see Hendrie, Diane
Harris, Ethel Wilson, 82, 75 n. 6, 108 n. 7,
    111 n. 56
Harris, Robert, 96, 111 n. 56

Hart, Kay, 75 n. 9
Hatgil, Paul, 109 n. 16
Heck, Al, 76 n. 22, 78 n. 36
Heickman, Mary, 117, 142
Hellman, Blanche, 87, 96, 97, 105
HemisFair '68, 90, 92, 94, 96-98, 113, 111
    n. 50
Hendrie, Diane, 117
Hendrie, Helen Marie, 87, 90, 94, 97, 98,
    102, 105, 113, 115-117, 121, 123, 127,
    128, 155, 162, 163, 183, 184
Henry, O., 31, 53 n. 91
Herff, Ferdinand, 27
Herff, Ferdinand Peter, 27, 55 n. 117
Hils, Robert, 172, 186
Hixon, Frederick C., 125
Hixon, Joan, 87, 89, 97, 110 n. 36
Holliday, Claire, 159, 172, 187
Holmgreen, John, 179 n. 12
Housing and Urban Development,
    Department of, 124, 111 n. 48, 140 n. 36
Houston Museum of Fine Arts, 181 n. 42
Hua, Phuong-Thao, 172
Hudson, Ursula. see under Ursuline Sisters
Hugman, Robert H.H., 110 n. 45
Hull House Art School, 64, 65, 77 n. 23
Humphrey, Steve, 128, 130, 186, 139 n. 26
Hundere, Alice, 100, 101
Huth, Theresa O'Farrell, 125, 135

Instituto Allende, 109 n. 16

Johnson, Ruth, 123, 125-128, 134, 136,
    137, 145, 147-151, 153, 158
Johnson, Stewart, 123
Jones, Essie, 59
Jones, Griff, 75 n. 8
Jones, Isabelle Callaghan, 59, 75 n. 8
Jordan, Floy Fontaine, 66, 157
Joske's of Texas, 96, 98, 99
Jung, Cho Ki, 172

Kampmann, J.H., 52 n. 80
Kaneko, Jun, 164
Kansas City Art Institute, 142
Keehn, Thomas, 78 nn. 33, 37
Kefauver, Lisa, 101
Keller, Jane, 106
Kenna, Michael, 164
Kersey, Diana, 175
Key, Rhoderick, 162
Kincaid, Josephine, 84
Kinzie, Margaret, 85

Know-Nothing (Party), 22
Koch, Augustus, 28, 29, 31, 53 n. 88
Kohnitz, Harvey, 186
Kvistad, Sandra Kay, 47

Lagagnina, Tom, 173
La Reunion, 50 n. 39
La Sala. *see under* Southwest School of Art
 and Craft
La Sirena, 88, 90, 110 n. 32
La Villita, 92-94, 98, 101, 105, 113, 123,
 127, 162, 185, 110 n. 36, 111 nn. 46,
 64, 139 n. 24
Lamb, Ellie, 173
Lamm, Fr. William, 46
Lance, Mike, 168
Lang, Maggie, 96
Lanier, Sidney, 31, 53 n. 91
Larsen, Jack Lenor, 162
Larsen, Marcie Baer, 132, 142
LaVilla-Havelin, Jim, 172, 188
Lawrie, Joe, 128
Learning About Learning, 100
Lee, Amy Freeman, 109 n. 23
Lehr, Walter G., Jr., 68
Lende, Bill, 155, 140 n. 45
Leo XIII, 33
Leopoldine Society, 6, 49 n. 17
Leven, Bishop Stephen, 76 n. 22
Lewis, Nat, 19, 53 n. 83
Lifshutz, Bernard, 168
Light, Patsy, 105
Linn, John Joseph, 2, 48 n. 2, 49 n. 8
Lipofsky, Marvin, 142
Louis, Saint, 49 n. 19
Lucey, Robert E. (archbishop of San
 Antonio), 44, 57, 61, 63, 69, 75 n. 9, 76
 n. 20, 77 n. 29
Lungkwitz, Hermann, 107 n. 1

McAllister, Clio, 120
McAllister, Edith, 89, 94, 123, 133, 134,
 155, 156, 166, 168, 183, 184, 111 n. 51,
 179 n. 15
McAllister, Walter, 68, 120, 77 n. 32
McCloskey, Mother Marie. *see under*
 Ursuline Sisters
McConkey, John, 159, 186
McCullough, Rev. John, 9, 10
MacDonald, David, 175
McFee, Henry Lee, 82, 108 n. 8
McNay, Marion, 82, 108 n. 10
McNutt, Amy Shelton, 127, 145, 147-151,
 153, 159
McNutt, V.H., 150
Madam Louie, 63
Maddux, Betty. *see* Coates, Elizabeth
 (Betty) Huth
Maddux, Sam, 139 n. 22
Madero [Evaristo], 24, 52 n. 71
Magruder, Hamilton, 94, 111 n. 46
Magruder, Lydia, 111 n. 46
Main Avenue High School, 53 n. 95
Marcella, Mother. *see under* Ursuline Sisters
Martin, Brooks, 134
Mata Ortiz, 171, 172
Mathis, Walter, 69, 122, 126, 179 n. 15
Matthews, Zelime, 137
Maverick, Lucy, 77 n. 24
Maverick, Maury, 92, 93, 101
Maverick-Clarke Lithography Company, 43,
 61, 55 n. 118, 181 n. 49
Maxham, Kay, 87, 97, 101, 105, 116, 117,
 159, 175, 185, 186
Meander, The, *see under* Ursuline Academy
Menger, Eleonore Lange, 76 nn. 12, 21
Menger, Gene, 105
Menger, Henry J., 76 nn. 12, 21
Menger, Linda, 105
Mijangos, Alberto, 172
Mill Race Art Studio, 84
Missoula Museum of Art, 181 n. 46
Momma Mac. *see* Amy Shelton McNutt
Monaghan, Sarah. *see* Ursuline Sisters: St.
 Antoine
Montsalvage, Rev. Ramon, 9
Mood, Martha, 105
Moore, Jeffrey, 159, 160, 162-165, 180 n.
 32
Morgan, Anne, 85, 109 n. 18
Morton, Cliff, 123
Mount St. Mary's College, 12
Mueller, Mother Anita. *see under* Ursuline
 Sisters
Municipal Auditorium, 41, 43, 54 n. 111
Murray, Monsignor P.J., 69
Museum School of Art, 82, 108 n. 8
Myers, Faleta, 97

National Bank of Commerce, 61, 63, 120,
 77 n. 30, 138 n. 17
Navarro, José Antonio, House 75 n. 4, 179
 n. 11
Navarro Street Bridge, 38
Naylor, Alice, 86
NEA (National Endowment for the Arts),

102, 128, 139 n. 27

Neal, Josie, 106

Negley, Carolyn Brown (Mrs. William), 116, 122, 125, 128, 130, 131, 153, 156, 138 n. 18, 139 nn. 31, 32

Negley, Laura Burleson (Mrs. Richard), 131, 139 n. 31

Negley, Nancy Brown (Mrs. Alfred), 87-90, 96, 100, 134, 135, 183, 184, 110 n. 37, 138 n. 18, 139 n. 22, 140 nn. 36, 44, 179 n. 11

Newbury, Lee, 154, 187

Newcomb College School of Art, 86

Newcomb, James Pearson, 22, 51 n. 65

Newman, Sarah, 101

Nottingham, Walter, 160

NYA (National Youth Administration), 82, 92, 101, 105, 111 n.64, 139 n. 24

O'Banion, Nance, 164

Odin, John Marie (archbishop of New Orleans), 1, 3-10, 12, 14-20, 22-24, 26, 27, 38, 175, 49 nn. 8, 14, 16, 19, 21, 50 nn. 23, 24, 33, 51 n. 64, 75 n. 8

Onderdonk, Julian, 81

Onderdonk, Robert Jenkins, 34

Oppenheimer, Jesse, 179 n. 15, 180 n. 25

Osborn, Frederick H., 139 n. 33

Owen, Paula Berg, 167, 169, 170, 187

Pace, Linda, 105, 106

Padilla, Lupe, 148, 149

Pagona, Victor, 186

Parrott, Alice Kagawa, 109 n. 16

Paschal, I.A., 19

Paseo del Rio San Antonio, 92, 93

Paul V, 17

Pauly, Henry, 31

Pawel, Nancy, 97, 106

Peery, Allison, 94

Penland School of Crafts, 142

Philips, Mary Walker, 142

Picante Paper Studio. *see under* Southwest School of Art and Craft

pisé de terre, 13, 14, 50 n. 37

Pius IX, 49 n.16

Poinsard Square, 66, 77 n. 30

Poinsard, Hannah, 15

Poinsard, Jules, 13-15, 58, 50 n. 39, 51 nn. 40, 41, 49

Poinsard's Folly, 15, 68, 75 n. 9

Portier, Lise. *see* Ursuline Sisters: St. Alexis

Pozo, Angelica, 175

Putnam County Products, 109 n. 18

Putnam, Margaret, 97

Quillin, Ellen Schulz, 82, 107 n. 6, 108 nn. 7, 8

Quillin, Roy, 107 n. 6

Ramsdell, Jacquelyn, 98

Ray, Harry R., 76 n. 17

Red Cross Arts and Skills Program, 84

Reitz, Don, 163

Richardson, Mother Mary Joseph. *see under* Ursuline Sisters

Ringgold, Faith, 164

River Walk, 92, 100

River Walk Advisory Commission, 69, 78 n. 34

Rivera, Diego, 77 n. 26

Riverside School, 53 n. 94

Robinson, Taylor, 109 n. 16

Rockefeller Collection, 179 n. 21

Rogers, John, 187

Romberg, Jim, 160

Ross, Harriet, 157

Rowden, Francine, 182 n. 64

RTC (Resolution Trust Corporation), 166, 181 nn. 52, 53

Russell, Naomi, 99, 144, 146, 178 n. 10

Sacred Heart Academy, 36, 37, 54 n. 101

St. Mary's Church, 12, 50 n. 27, 52 n.75

St. Mary's Hall, 28

St. Mary's of the Barrens Seminary, 2, 7

St. Mary's School, 20

St. Michael's School, 36, 54 n. 101

St. Philip's College, 142

St. Ursula, Company (Order) of, 17

Samuel, William G.M., 9, 107 n. 1

San Antonio Art Institute, 84, 108 n. 13, 182 n. 63

San Antonio Art League, 81, 82, 84, 86, 87, 90, 77 n. 32, 107 nn. 4, 5, 110 n. 30

San Antonio College, 92

San Antonio Conservation Society:
    founding, 64
    Ursuline Academy and:
        initial interest, 58, 60, 66, 75 nn. 5, 6
        initial proposal, 68, 69, 77 n. 32
        initial purchase, 70, 78 n. 37
        Fire Department award, 73
        restoration of buildings, 118, 124, 133, 138 n. 11, 140 n. 38
        subsequent purchase, 118

sale of property, 133-135, 151
site use, 74, 114-116, 119
Ursuline inches, 73, 74
San Antonio de Valero Mission. *see* Alamo
San Antonio Housing Authority, 74
San Antonio Independent School District,
100-102
San Antonio Museum Association, 82
San Antonio Museum of Art, 179 n. 21
San Antonio Printmakers, 82, 107 n. 7
San Antonio River Authority, 111 n. 48
San Antonio Symphony League, 90
San Antonio Water Works, 82, 108 n. 8
San Fernando Church, 3, 4, 12
San Fernando Cemetery #1, 55 n. 117
San José Mission, 3, 82, 78 n. 39, 107 n. 4,
108 n. 7, 111 n. 56
San José Pottery, 108 n. 7, 111 n. 56
San Juan Mission, 3
San Pedro Springs, 12, 54 n. 103
Sanders, Regina, 172
Sangre de Cristo Arts and Conference
Center, 153
Santa Rosa Infirmary, 15
SANYO (San Antonio Neighborhood
Youth Organization), 123, 139 n. 20
Saturday Morning Discovery. *see under*
Southwest School of Art and Craft
Saucedo, Alberto, 172
Schmitt, Francis C., 23, 26, 52 n. 75
Schoenig, Jean, 97, 105, 112 n. 67
School for American Craftsmen, 86
Sears, Roebuck and Company, 61, 72, 164-
166, 168, 171, 55 n. 118, 76 n. 15, 181
nn. 49, 53
Seeligson, Ramona, 110 n. 39
Seguin, Erasmo, 49 n. 14
Seguin, Juan, 2, 49 n. 14
Sharpe, Florida Tunstall, 59
Shelton, Caroline, 96, 98, 142
Shook, Janet, 87, 110 n. 32
Sigwald, Pablo, 172
Sigwald, Vicki, 172
Simons, Sally, 96
Slick, Tom, 110 n. 30
Smith, Bertie, 97, 154
Smith, Dennis, 142, 156, 159, 172, 175, 186
Smith, Harwood K., 76 n. 17
Society for the Propagation of the Faith, 6,
8, 20, 49 n. 17
Soldner, Paul, 128, 130, 142, 186, 139 n. 26
Soto, Ishmael, 96
Southwest Craft Center. *see* Southwest

School of Art and Craft
Southwest Foundation for Research and
Education, 156, 180 n. 24
Southwest School of Art and Craft:
Adele and Jack Frost Garden 151, 156,
140 n. 41
Amy Shelton McNutt Garden Room,
150, 159, 180 n. 32
Angel Tapestry, 137
artist-in-residence program, 117, 128, 130,
160, 185, 139 nn. 26, 27
Big Craft Deal, 100, 101, 102
Champagne Under the Stars, 97-100
Copper Kitchen, 127, 145, 148-150,
153, 157, 159, 179 n. 11, 180 n. 41
Creative Arts School, 117, 169, 185
curriculum, 102, 103, 105, 128, 132,
142, 155, 159, 162, 164. 166, 168,
172, 185-187
Edith McAllister Ceramics Studio, 133,
156, 160, 166
Elizabeth Huth Coates Chapel, 134,
135-137, 139 n. 22, 140 n. 44
Emily Edwards Room (Gallery), 66,
157-159, 180 n. 32
Fiesta Arts Fair, 144, 146, 147
Folk Craft Experience, 144-147, 178 nn.
8, 9
founding, 87-89
La Casita, 101-103, 105, 106, 185, 186,
139 n. 21
La Sala, 157
La Villita Gallery, 90, 93-98, 101, 103,
105, 113, 162, 185, 110 n. 39, 111
n. 54
name change, 169, 170
Navarro Campus, 166-173, 175, 188,
181 n. 53
Picante Paper Studio, 186
Pickle Project, 99
Russell Hill Rogers Gallery, 171, 172, 188
Saturday Morning Discovery, 100-102,
115, 128, 154, 166, 175, 185, 179 n. 15
Ursuline Academy acquisition and
renovation, 114-118, 120-127, 130-
135, 153, 155, 138 n. 11
Ursuline Angels, 135, 140 n. 45
Visitors Center Museum, 173, 188
students, pictures of, 103, 105, 128,
142, 145, 154, 160, 175, 177
workshop program, 160, 164
Sowall, John, 109 n. 23
Spanish Governors Palace, 75 n. 4

Staffel, Rudolf, 82, 107 n. 6
Stanley, Thomas E., 78 n. 33
State Art School, 107 n. 3
Steinfeldt, Cecilia, 85
Steves, Marshall, 110 n. 32
Steves, Patsy, 114, 110 n. 32
Straus, David, 180 n. 23
Streiber, Mary Drought, 68
Sullivan, William C., 38, 54 n. 110
Summa, Tim, 172, 186
Syfan, Helen Edwards, 59, 63, 64

Templeton, Eva, 187
Texas Arts Alliance, 163
Texas Commission on the Arts, 163
Texas Commission on the Arts and
    Humanities, 187
Texas Designer Craftsmen, 86
Texas Historical Commission, 124, 125
Texas State Ceramic and Textile Exhibit,
    84, 108 n. 13
Texas State Crafts Exhibit, 84, 108 n. 14
Thomas, Ann, 95, 96, 163
Tiemann, Caroline, 142
Timon, Fr. John, 2-4, 8, 48 nn. 5, 7, 49 n. 14
Tobin, John, 107 n. 5
Tobin, Margaret (Mag), 66, 100, 101, 153,
    179 n. 15
Tobin, Peggy, 70, 114
Todd, Dena, 138 n. 9
Treut, Joyce, 101, 105
Trouard, Constance. see Ursuline Sisters:
    St. Marie, Mother
Tucker, Stevie, 96, 111 n. 57
Tunstall, Warwick, 53 n. 83
Twiggs, David E., 23

University of the Americas Graduate
    School, 142
Unlimited Potential Teacher Resource
    Center, 100, 101
Ursa, 72, 78 n. 42
Ursula, Saint, 17, 46
Urschel, Charles, 120, 121, 128, 110 n. 30
Urschel, Elizabeth (Betty), 87, 89, 90, 96,
    97, 115, 121, 128, 141, 183, 184, 110
    nn. 29, 30
Ursel, 72
Ursuline Academy:
    Angel Arches, 41, 47
    Angels' Hall, 40, 41, 72
    charter, State, 31
    closing of downtown campus, 44, 57

construction of, 13-15, 23, 26-28, 31,
    41, 53 n. 90, 54 nn. 103, 112
curriculum, 20, 28, 29, 33, 46
founding of, 4, 5, 7, 8, 10, 16, 18-20
grotto, Lady of Lourdes, 33, 41, 42, 152
new location of, 43, 57, 61, 63, 70
Meander, The, 34, 38, 41, 42
Poor School, 54 n. 96
sale of downtown campus, 58, 60, 61,
    63, 66, 68, 70, 76 nn. 12, 15, 17, 20,
    21, 22, 78 nn. 36, 37
Select School, 40, 41, 72, 53 nn. 90, 96
Serviam pin, 46
students, pictures of, 31, 34, 35, 45, 47,
    64, 178
Ursuline Addition, 38, 39
Ursuline Angels. see under Southwest
    School of Art and Craft
Ursuline Coat of Arms, 17
Ursuline Convent, New Orleans, 16
Ursuline Sisters:
    Angela, 18
    Anita Mueller, Mother, 57, 60, 61
    Augustine Joseph, 13
    Marcella, Mother, 47
    Marie McCloskey, Mother, 63, 69, 70,
        78 n. 36
    Mary Augustine Joseph, 19, 20, 130
    Mary Joseph Richardson, Mother, 70
    Mary Magdalen (Rudecinda de la
        Garza), Mother, 20, 28, 31, 53 n. 85
    Mary Patrick Joseph (Walshe), 18-20,
        51 n. 50
    Mary Rose, Mother, 44
    St. Alexis (Lise Portier), 18, 19
    St. Antoine (Sarah Monaghan), 18
    St. Isidore (Rosalie Entienne), 18
    St. Marie, 18
    St. Marie Trouard (Constance Trouard),
        Mother, 18, 19, 24
    Ursula Hudson, Mother, 33, 38
    Xavier, 18

van Baarle, Els, 172
Vance House, 75 n. 4
Van Dyke Art Association, 81, 107 n. 3
Vargas, Kathy, 130, 139 n. 29

Wachter, Merle, 142, 153
Wagner, Cyrus, 92, 119, 111 n. 48
Wagner, Jearnine, 100
Walshe, Ned, 18, 51 n. 50
Washington State University, 181 n. 46

Watson, Elsa Buss, 79 n. 43
Webb, Aileen Osborn, 85, 86, 109 nn. 17,
    23, 139 n. 33
Wegman, William, 161, 163
Weincek, Nelle Lee, 70
Welch, Jane, 105
Wheeler, Ethel, 157
Whitehead, Beck, 159, 172, 186
Willson Metals Studio, 164
Willson, Margaret Bosshardt Pace, 86, 87,
    92, 94, 96, 98, 105, 113, 116, 170, 183,
    184, 186, 109 n. 26, 111 nn. 50, 51, 138
    n. 2, 182 n. 63
Wilson, Madelyn, 117
Winn, Robert K., 88-90, 96, 98, 116, 108 n.
    13, 109 nn. 16, 21, 179 n. 21
Witte Museum, 82, 84-88, 108 nn. 8, 10, 13,
    110 n. 39
WPA (Works Progress Administration), 44,
    92
Wright, Tom, 128, 130, 185, 186, 139 n. 28

Yamada, Shinman, 172, 175

Zemlin, Therese, 173
Zilker, Sandra, 164

Acknowledgments

When I was invited to write the sesquicentennial history of the "school on the river," built as San Antonio's Ursuline Academy and now home to the Southwest School of Art and Craft, I was struck by the story's important themes that parallel my own life. Raised a Catholic, I became a historian, an advocate of historic preservation, and a lover of art. While writing this story it was intriguing to understand how these threads wove together over 150 years to preserve and perpetuate this unique place that we celebrate today.

My thanks go to all of the founders of the Southwest School of Art and Craft, for they have recorded the organization's history on tape and through their collected papers. I would like to especially thank Helen Marie Hendrie and Maggie Block who were always available to answer a question or gather a group to collect remembrances. The school's rich history has been made available to this writer (and to all interested researchers) through the tireless efforts of Ellie Lamb and her committee who have labored to establish one of San Antonio's fine archival collections of organizational papers. This work was made possible through the generosity of the late Floy Fontaine Jordan, who became devoted to the Ursuline and its preservation through the inspiration of her aunt, Emily Edwards. Valuable assistance has also been provided by the Southwest School of Art and Craft's director, Paula Owen, and her staff including former Director of Public Programs, Tracy Baker-White, Public Relations Coordinator, Mike Pecen, and Director of Development, Ed Conroy.

Generous help has come from my colleagues and fellow history lovers including Sister Rosemary Meiman, Archivist, Ursuline Provincialate; Jo Myler and Frank Faulkner of the San Antonio Public Library's. Texana/Genealogy Department; Elaine Davis, director of the D.R.T. Library and her staff members, Dora Elizondo Guerra, Martha Utterback, and Warren Stricker; San Antonio Conservation Society librarians, Marianna Jones and the late Nelle Lee Weincek; Brother Edward Loch of the Catholic Archives of San Antonio; Tom Shelton of the Institute of Texan Cultures; Rebecca Huffstutler of the Witte Museum; Dr. Donald E. Everett, Trinity University, Professor Emeritus of History; Kinga Perzynska and Susan Eason of the Catholic Archives of Texas; and Dr. Francois Lagarde, Dr. Richard Cleary, and Dr. Betje Klier who guided me through the intricacies of the French in Texas.

Final thanks go to Lewis Fisher of Maverick Publishing Company, book designer Barbara Whitehead and graphic designers Donna Baxter and John Crain who shared their advice and counsel; Michaele and David Haynes who are stern but patient critics; and my husband Fred Pfeiffer who shares my love of San Antonio's 19th century landmarks along the San Antonio River.